Loss and

what it taught me about

Living

A MEMOIR OF LOVE, GRIEF, HOPE AND HEALING

TRACEY CORBETT-LYNCH

WITH RALPH RIEGEL

Gill Books

Gill Books

Hume Avenue

Park West

Dublin 12

www.gillbooks.ie

Gill Books is an imprint of M.H. Gill and Co.

9780717194674

Design and print origination by O'K Graphic Design, Dublin

Edited by Neil Burkey

Printed by CPI Group (UK) Ltd, Croydon, CRO 4YY

This book is typeset in 12/20 pt Sabon.

The paper used in this book comes from the wood pulp of sustainably managed forests.

> This book is not intended as a substitute for the medical advice of a physician. The reader should consult a doctor or mental health professional if they feel it necessary.

A CIP catalogue record for this book is available from the British Library.

5 4 3 2 1

Tracey Corbett-Lynch is mother to a blended family of four children. Dean and Adam are her two eldest with her husband David. Jack and Sarah are her brother Jason Corbett's children, whom she won custody of after Jason was killed in North Carolina in 2015.

Ralph Riegel is Southern Correspondent for the *Irish Independent* and a regular contributor to RTÉ, BBC and Virgin Media. Previous books include *Afraid of the Dark: The Tragic Story of Robert Holohan*; *Shattered: Killers Do Time, Victims' Families Do Life*; *My Brother Jason*; and *A Dream of Death*. He lives in Cork.

To my four children, Dean, Adam, Jack and Sarah.
Remember that our love will always exist, even when
I no longer do.

CONTENTS

INTRODUCTION: MAKING SENSE OF THE SENSELESS

Why me? – two small words with incredibly destructive, spirit-sapping power. How do I know? Because I have uttered them often enough as I have reeled from the loss of loved ones in life, raged at how unfair the world could be, cried bitter tears at how awful things could happen to good people, and felt frightened by how helpless and insignificant we can be in this world. I had come to realise that I was helpless to change the events that had irrevocably transformed my life and the lives of those I loved.

Murder, cancer, Covid-19, an asthma attack and heart attacks – I have lost loved ones to all five. Although I didn't know it until years later, I was a twin who had lost my sibling before I was born. So it is fair to say that, almost from the beginning, I've had to deal with a sense of loss in my life, and have discovered that there is an entire community out there united by grief and pain.

If you're holding this book in your hands, you've probably endured something similar. Without warning, your life suddenly became a series of 'before and after' events. That's how it was for me. There was Tracey before all these losses, and then there was the Tracey who emerged after grief struck with all its might.

Perhaps you're just starting out on your own grief journey, and are struggling to understand where that frustrating, painful path will lead and what your final destination will be. Will you find comfort? Maybe some hope? Or at the very least some temporary escape from the terrible aching pain that the loss of a loved one can inflict on every waking moment? Is there any end to the almost physical pain that such grief brings?

Grief comes in many different shapes and forms. I've primarily dealt with the loss of loved ones, sometimes in the most appalling and tragic of circumstances. But you don't have to lose a loved one to death to grieve; grief can strike from the premature ending of a career, from the loss of a faculty, from the ending of a marriage or relationship, from the debilitating aftermath of a medical condition and even from the ending of a friendship. Many of the emotions we experience, such as fear, anxiety, loneliness and self-doubt, are precisely the same.

The recovery principles are very much the same as well. The first thing to remember is that you're not alone. When all else fails you, never forget that. Across the world, tens of thousands of people at this very moment are feeling like you feel right now. Their language, religion and skin colour don't make their grief and pain any greater or lesser than yours. It is very, very important to remember that you are not alone in feeling like this.

For generations, human beings have struggled to make sense of loss and grief – the Egyptian pyramids, the great temples of Greece and Rome and the megalithic tombs dotted across the Irish landscape are ancient methods of trying to make sense of the cycles of life and to pay tribute to someone who has died.

Across human history, a reverence for lost ancestors is a recurring theme. Ancient peoples used their own tributes in stone and metal to honour lost loved ones, from small carved statuettes right through to vast monuments that, thousands of years later, are so awe-inspiring that they take the breath away. For some, such as kings, pharaohs and emperors, the scale and beauty of the monuments were their own pitch for immortality, at least in terms of never being forgotten. For a humble peasant, it might be a simple stone or a carved wooden post, raised to commemorate a beloved parent, wife, husband, son or daughter. But the aim is the same.

Our modern world is no different, but instead of building great temples for lost loved ones, we build more modest memorials, in cemeteries and remembrance halls, or even at the roadside – a tribute left by someone heartbroken at the loss of a loved one in a road traffic accident.

On a much more intimate scale, we also build memorials out of paper – such as this book. We put up social media tribute pages or lovingly make memory boxes, lest we forget the cherished details of the person we miss. All of which help us to cope, to heal and to return to life with our loved one firmly entrenched in our memory. We take cherished mementoes of a loved one – watches, rings, necklaces – wrap them carefully and preserve them for the next generation.

In my case, my mother's wedding ring went to my sister Marilyn before she, with my dad's approval, gave it to my son Dean for his wedding. A symbol of my mother's life and love was passed on to another generation. But the point is that the need for comfort, for connection, for understanding and for remembrance across the generations is as powerful today as it was a millennia ago.

Years ago, I read that grief is the price we pay for love and, as I mourned the loss of loved ones over the years, it had always seemed to me that whoever came up with that statement was full of crap. Not for one moment did I agree with the sentiment involved. I found it offered no comfort and merely reminded me what I had lost – and it hinted that, having loved, now was the time to pay the price for it. Where is the comfort in that? It felt like we faced punishment for having loved deeply and dearly.

In my life, I've lost a twin; had an adored sister-in-law suffer a fatal asthma attack in the prime of her life; had a brother murdered by his second wife and father-in-law; been caught in a seven-year legal nightmare over my family's campaign for justice for him; had a cherished brother-in-law die; and, then, just when I thought I had coped with all that life could possibly throw at me, had the Covid-19 pandemic claim my adored mother.

In 2006, my brother Jason lost his wife, Margaret 'Mags' Fitzpatrick, to a sudden asthma attack. She was only 31 years old, and her death left Jason to raise two children under the age of three on his own. Mags wasn't just my sister-in-law – she was also one of my closest friends.

The death of Mags drove me into a deep depression, one that I struggled with for years afterwards. How could someone so young, so vivacious and with so much to live for be taken so suddenly? Without warning, it created a huge imbalance in my life. The unfairness of it struck at the deepest part of my psyche, and I was reminded of the terrible cost of her loss on a daily basis, as I saw my brother try to raise his children, Jack and Sarah.

Watching him attempting to make sense of a life without his soulmate left me feeling so powerless. I had to learn through hard-won experience that, while you can't lessen a person's grief by taking it on yourself, you *can* help them live with the burden of loss through friendship, support and encouragement.

In 2007, my mother-in-law, Norah, died in tragic circumstances when she fell down the stairs of her Limerick home after suffering a heart attack. Norah was 64 years old, and an active woman who took great pride in her family, and was there for us during one of the darkest periods of our own lives. To add to the tragedy, it was just one month before her youngest son was due to get married in Italy, a day she was eagerly preparing for.

In August 2015, my brother Jason was murdered in the United States, where he had set up home with his Tennessee-born second wife, Molly Martens.

Molly had moved to Limerick to work as a nanny for Jason's two children, Jack and Sarah, and quickly got involved in a relationship with my brother. They married in June 2011 despite my misgivings that Jason was vulnerable due to his loneliness and ongoing grief over the loss of Mags. I wasn't the only one who was worried, and several of Jason's great friends had tried to plead with him to stall the wedding.

Just four years after the wedding, Jason was killed by Molly and her father, Tom Martens, in a calculated attack I am convinced revolved around control of his two children. The brutality of the murder was shocking – but it was the callous betrayal of a devoted family man that proved so wounding.

We waited two years for the murder trial, and then, once convictions and 25-year sentences were imposed, the appeal process began. Almost seven years after Jason's death, we are still trapped in the meat grinder of the judicial system, still waiting for closure. It is as if the wound of Jason's brutal killing slowly begins to heal, only for it to be ripped open again by fresh legal challenges.

We have to watch and listen as details of the horrific crime are replayed again and again on radio and on TV, as well as in newspapers and magazines. For seven years it has been like being trapped in an unending nightmare with no escape and no opportunity to protect yourself.

Jack and Sarah were left orphaned, and my family was left bereft. It shook the very foundations of my world. Jason wasn't so much my brother as one of my best friends. We were deeply involved in each other's lives – we holidayed together, he stayed with us when he came home to Ireland, we organised weekends away as families, and Jason liked nothing more than playing golf with my husband. Jason was only 39 years old when he was killed.

In the middle of the battle for justice for Jason, my brother-in-law Kevin died of cancer in Florida in August 2016. Kevin had been a pillar of strength for us when Jason was killed in North Carolina, providing invaluable support during our time in the US.

My husband, Dave, had also suffered the death of his father, John, when he was 19. John had been in the UK working as an engineer on the M21 motorway. Dave had been with him the previous weeks, and John's death was devastating to his wife, Norah, and their young children. John was just 50 years old, and, after his death, was diagnosed with cancer which was present in multiple locations and which had an unknown origin. Most likely it started as stomach cancer. Years later, the tragedy was repeated when John's son – Kevin – would also die from cancer aged just 49.

Kevin had a wonderful sense of fun and humour – in our darkest times, he still somehow managed to lighten our mood. It was a devastating blow, as he had been a rock for us, as had Dave's sister, Linda, and his brothers Paul and Michael – we drew such enormous strength from knowing we had their support to draw on when so far from home.

In May 2020, my mother contracted Covid-19. Our family had gone to incredible lengths to help her and my elderly father safely cocoon from the virus, but, sadly, it was in vain. I held her hand just hours before she passed. Witnessing the fear, loneliness and isolation of a coronavirus death is a deeply raw, almost visceral pain. Only someone who has experienced a Covid-19 loss will know what I am talking about.

My mother was 80 years old and, but for the pandemic,

would have had years of life left to her. In the cruellest possible fashion, our family was not even able to properly say goodbye to my dying mother because of virus protocols in place in Ireland at the height of the pandemic. Imagine not being able to hold the hand of and offer words of comfort to the woman who gave you life. I wanted to look into her eyes to somehow convey the love she had showered on us all her life, to offer her comfort and solidarity when she needed it most. Even the simplest act of holding her hand, a physical touch, just to say, *you loved and were loved, and your life mattered to us.*

I should have been honouring her life, giving her strength by my physical presence while knowing that her time on this earth was now a matter of hours and days. How many families said their final goodbyes to loved ones through Perspex partitions or the masks and visors of plastic personal protective equipment? Some even said goodbye via the screens of tablets and smartphones. Even now as I write this, more than two years later, just mentioning it brings an ache to my heart. Truth be told, I'm still on my grief journey. The purpose of this book is to show that, while the journey may be long and you will face setbacks, if you face the reality of life, love and of loss, the pain at each station along the way can be lessened.

I outline these losses not to explain my grief but, rather, to explain how I found my own way to celebrate these lives

– to arrive at a point where I am thankful that I had these bright, wonderful human beings in my life. I'm not writing to seek sympathy or compassion. Neither am I going to claim that there aren't days when I miss them with every fibre of my being – that there won't be days when a smell, a song or a memory brings tears to my eyes. Rather, I want to assure you that such devastating losses can be coped with, and that, despite everything, you can find a way to move forward and live an enriching life where the memory of your loved one is a treasure and not a burden.

So while I am not an expert on emotional behaviour, and I don't profess to have psychological qualifications, I do know about grief – from hard-worn personal experience. The reason for this book is that I struggled to make sense of the losses I had suffered and was desperately looking for something to help. But I couldn't find it – at least not in a simple-to-access book about how to cope with grief and practical things to do to ease the pain.

I realised that there is a world of pain out there that I was totally unaware of. After Jason's death, I worked with my cousin, Nuala Galvin, and my friend, Richard Lynch, to set up a Facebook group to campaign for justice for my brother. It introduced me to vast numbers of people who were themselves struggling to cope with loss, many having lost loved ones to violent crime. They wanted to help me and my family in a bid to help ease their own pain. What developed was a community of people left bruised by grief but who wanted to share compassion, solidarity and hope.

On 31 October 2021, Nuala suffered a devastating loss when her stepson, Adam, who was aged just 22, was killed in a road traffic accident. The young man was critically injured in a single-vehicle collision and was pronounced dead at the scene. Adam, who was from Limerick, was a final year student of Pharmaceutical and Forensic Science at Limerick Institute of Technology, and was a wonderful young man.

In deciding to write this book, I wanted to tell my story of how I coped – and to try to offer some answers as to how you can learn to live with the blinding pain of grief. I wanted to provide the answers I had found to some of the questions I had asked myself when confronted with tragic losses. What can you do to lessen the pain? How can you make sense of the senseless? How do you get on with life when there are times you can't recognise the life you are left with? Is there anything that can fill the aching void once occupied by a person who effortlessly made your world so special? Someone who you realise is no longer there, except in cherished memories.

After the first tragedy we suffered as a family, I needed a simple 'how to' guide to help me cope – to be able to put one foot in front of the other until it didn't hurt to think about the aftermath of the loss I now faced. Basically, I needed to learn about coping and to educate myself about grief and develop a toolbox for carrying and managing this grief. Without intending to, I launched myself on a journey of self-discovery.

I didn't want an academic book or a spiritual volume. I didn't particularly want to understand the deeper meaning of the cycles of life. What I desperately wanted were suggestions about things to do to lessen the sense of loss: shared stories and advice for what to do when the pain got so bad that I wanted to scream at the heavens. In the middle of my pain, I wanted to know what practical things others had done to cope with their grief – to be able to function and face the challenges of a new day. What had other people done to ease their grief until the burden became enough to cope with on a day-to-day basis?

This book is the road map of my grief journey. It is my story – the things that worked for me along the way, the systems I put in place to cope with the heartache and to slowly find a path to recovery. And, equally as important, I have also included an outline of the things that didn't help me – the things I tried which I derived little or no comfort from. This is how I managed to find the strength to cope. At the end of each chapter, I've included a 'lesson' to recentre and focus you on your journey.

One of the hardest things to do in life is to look at yourself as you really are – flaws and all. To recognise who we truly are is to appreciate our strengths *and* our vulnerabilities. I learned the importance of having a wellness plan to fall back on when the crap hits the fan. Which, let's face it, happens often enough for me that I would be foolish not to have some contingency coping plan in place.

There is no magical process of transformation or creation. For me, there is a combined approach that nudges me from heartbreak to hope and requires a very special alchemy – and a bit of hard work and dedication. Our experiences shape how we view life. Those experiences can change. So can our responses to trauma. I don't believe that there is just one thing that can heal us – at least that is not what I have experienced.

It is a blended approach that has worked in keeping me connected, offering me refuge and helping me find healing. It involved a constant refocusing on the here and now and all that life has to offer, even in the harshest of environments. At some points after the death of a loved one, I have experienced physical pain. I was left so lonely, distraught, isolated and hopeless that I genuinely wondered if I would ever find my way back to being the happy, confident Tracey I once was.

I'll admit there were times when I felt as if grief was a tsunami about to overwhelm me. There were days when I felt as vulnerable and damaged as it is possible for a human being to feel. But I held all the tighter to the things I'll outline in the coming chapters – and arrived at a point where I realised that the sun does shine, that life can be lived with a smile and I can remember those I lost with a chuckle over a humorous memory or even a tear at an anniversary or birthday.

No two grief journeys are the same. That is very important to state at the outset. But some of the stations along the route are the same – and I hope the following pages offer you some comfort on your path to recovery.

REMINDER

Never, ever forget that you are not alone – help, support and a sympathetic, listening ear are there if you choose to reach out to them.

I

MY LOST TWIN

was 12 years old when, unwittingly, a simple childhood accident changed my entire outlook on life. Until then, I had been a typical youngster, oblivious to the concept of loss or grief. To my innocent eyes, life was a great adventure with no consequences to be overly concerned about. Afterwards, I came to realise just how precarious life can be – and how inexplicable events can be the difference between life and death, relief and tragedy.

I was one of the middle children of a typical Irish working-class family. My parents, John and Rita, lived in Janesboro, a suburb developed on the outskirts of Limerick during the boom of the 1960s in Ireland. My family taught me so much about the meaning of love, life, resilience in the face of the most difficult circumstances and the delicate threads of a lifetime of experiences that became the steel support wires that bound us together to face our futures with hope.

Looking back, I feel I had a blessed childhood. It wasn't easy at the time and, as a family, we didn't have much in the material sense. I realise now the hardships my parents faced, as well as the extraordinary efforts they made to raise us and give us every chance at a bright future. My parents married in 1960 and, Ireland being the ultra-conservative country it was at the time, my mother had no choice but to quit her job at a local Limerick firm. She had no say in the matter, such was the era she lived in and the view society had towards women. In Ireland in the 1950s and 1960s, a married woman's place was in the home – not in the workplace. As a result, my mother's life would become her husband and children, and we benefited from the warmth and kindness of her all-encompassing love and care over the decades.

My father worked as a driver for an oil firm, and his passion was his wife and children. It wasn't the perfect job back then, but while Dad worked there we had food on the table and a relatively comfortable life within our community.

Some of my most cherished memories are of playing games in the sitting room, and the happy times gathered in front of our black-and-white television set as the entire family sat transfixed, watching the hit programmes of the era, including *Charlie's Angels*, *Magnum PI*, *The Riordans* and, later, *Glenroe*. There were never rows about what programmes to watch, because there was only one channel. The rows began when we children were ordered to bed because we had school the following day, or because my parents had decided that a late-night film wasn't suitable viewing for us – maybe they knew there would be a kissing scene or, worse still, it was a 1950s vampire film that they were concerned would prevent us from sleeping. Looking back now, those films would likely seem tame in the extreme!

We were a very tight-knit family back then and were all involved in each other's lives. Like our neighbours, we didn't exactly have an excess of money. My parents generally had to save or borrow to buy any major items they needed for the home, such as a refrigerator, a cooker or even furniture. But, thanks to their hard work, we never went without. The Ireland of the 1960s and 1970s had virtually all families in a similar position, and there wasn't the apparent wealth gap that has emerged in society since.

To this day, I associate our Janesboro home with the sound of laughter and the smell of my mother's wonderful cooking. Sunday was a special day, because my mother ensured dinner was that bit extra-special. I can't believe she achieved so much with so little. We had a large back garden, and Dad would grow potatoes, cabbage, onions, lettuce and strawberries to help reduce grocery bills. For us children, the dessert on Sunday was something we looked forward to from Thursday.

There was a sense of community that we all took for granted. It was very much a working-class suburb that we grew up in – sport and playing outdoors were the dominant themes of almost every child's life. We didn't have expensive computer game consoles. Instead, we had the vast outdoors – nature's playground was on our doorstep, where our imaginations could run riot. There was a gang of us that would play bulldog and have innocent fun over the summer months. We all still have a WhatsApp group and keep in touch. Almost inevitably, we reminisce about the good old days, and it reminds me of the happier times in my life. Keeping in touch with childhood friends helps keep you grounded.

Luckily, we lived just a stone's throw from sprawling fields and woodland that I was convinced was truly magical. We could play princes and princesses, cowboys and Indians, hide and seek or, my personal favourite, games that involved nature itself.

I was a bit of a tomboy. I didn't give an inch to my brothers – I was fully capable of fighting my corner, and refused to be excluded from their play and relegated to what they termed 'girls' games'. There wasn't a tree I wouldn't climb, a stream I wouldn't jump across or a challenge I would refuse. I was blessed with a wonderful group of friends – first among them, my sister and brothers.

One of my favourite childhood games was trapping wild animals and then releasing them safely after having studied them at close hand. In our eyes, we were budding rivals of Sir David Attenborough, whose nature programmes we adored on the TV. We never had any success with rabbits or squirrels

– they were far too quick and cunning for us – but we devised a simple trap for hungry birds. We would use a bit of string, a stick to hold the trap open and then a simple make-shift cage of netting or wire. But it only worked if we placed the trap on a rooftop where the crows, pigeons or starlings felt they were safe to land and feed.

One day, when I was 12, I was playing with friends and we were setting up a trap for a bird. It was my turn to set the trap and, without thinking, I clambered up onto the shed roof in our back garden. Just as I went to prepare the trap, I stumbled and lost my footing. For a few seconds, I struggled to regain my balance and thought I would fall some 5 metres to earth. Luckily, I managed to avoid the edge of the roof and recovered my footing just in time to avoid disaster. My friends stared open-mouthed up at me, suddenly realising the danger. I got a terrible fright, but my first inclination was to grin at my friends below in a false display of bravado.

Unfortunately for me, my mother had been doing her housework and happened to be at the back window, from where she saw everything that happened, and immediately raced outside. Just one look at her face and I realised I was in deep trouble and needed to get back down to the safety of the garden immediately. She was livid – or so I thought. My friends scattered and, when I clambered down from the shed, I thought I was facing a stern rebuke and possibly even being banished indoors.

Instead, to my surprise, I realised that my mother was deeply upset. For a moment, I thought she was going to cry. I was confused. I adored my mother, and the last thing I wanted to do was to upset her, but I was young and foolish. She ordered me into the kitchen and then sat down beside me. With shock, I realised that her hands were trembling and that she was fighting back tears.

'Do you know you could have been killed?' she blurted out.

I lowered my eyes to the floor, shamefaced, and simply nodded, galled at having upset my mother.

'I thought you were going to fall. I got a terrible fright. I don't know what I would do if I lost you too.'

Embarrassed as I was, the word 'too' registered with me.

I looked up at my mother, and she could see the puzzlement spreading on my face. We had a happy family, and I knew of no one we had lost. Quite inexplicably, I felt a little twinge or ping in my breastbone. My brother Wayne had been quite ill when he was born but had rallied and become as rambunctious and healthy as his twin brother, Jason. I was too young to even know that at the time.

'What do you mean, Mam?' I asked her. I have no idea why she answered me; perhaps it was the shock of what she had just seen on the roof of the garden shed. Maybe she recognised the tomboy in me and wanted to curb my more adventurous instincts for my own good. I was wilful and stubborn and hungry for adventure. My mother stared at me for a moment, and then she uttered the words that, though I didn't realise it at the time, were my introduction to the concept of grief.

'I don't know what I would do, Tracey, if you fell and were hurt. I couldn't bear the thought of losing you. Because you were a twin, and I lost your other twin,' she explained. I was shocked and utterly perplexed. It was the first time I had heard I was a twin, just like Wayne and Jason. But what had happened to my twin?

My mother refused to say more but, years later, she explained that she was pregnant with twins when she felt unwell and was taken to see a doctor. Instantly, the doctor knew something was seriously wrong. Not long afterwards, my mother miscarried a baby. Somehow, I held on and avoided the fate of my sibling. When I was born, there were no complications, and I was a happy, healthy baby, to the relief of my parents.

I always wondered about my twin. It is very difficult to explain the sense of missing something that you never really had. I tried to get my mother to tell me more, but she steadfastly refused any further discussion of what happened.

I don't know at what stage of her pregnancy she miscarried my twin. I don't even know the gender of the baby that was lost. It's a strange sensation to realise you have lost a twin and not even know if you are mourning a brother or a sister. Bursting with questions, I knew I wasn't going to be given any answers because of the pain for my mother.

Years later, as a mother myself, I realise and empathise with my mother's situation. At that time there was no counselling or support other than her family. Back then, some things were just carried, and not spoken about. I can understand the awful predicament my mother found herself in. She was confronted by the overwhelming grief over the loss of a baby and the sheer relief of another baby being born healthy, defying the odds to cling to life. It was a study in terrible contrasts. Her focus was on caring for me, as well as her other five children. She had one healthy twin to nurse, so I suppose grieving for her lost twin was somehow postponed. But that near-tragedy on the shed roof demonstrated to me that my mother had never forgotten the tiny baby lost to her.

The knowledge of this changed my outlook on life. After that day, I realised that loss and grief were as much a part of life as happiness and laughter. It may sound over-dramatic, but it was as if one part of my childhood ended that day and the concept of death suddenly became real for me. I never forgot my lost twin. To this day, almost 40 years on, I often think of my lost sibling who, for the first 12 years of my life, I never even knew existed. But the cat was out of the bag. I had been introduced to death and the concept of losing someone. I understand now why my mother acted as she did in effectively shutting down the subject. It was something she wanted to deal with and not involve me in. I know now this was done to protect me from being frightened by the concept of death and loss at such a young and impressionable age.

But what my mam didn't realise was that Pandora's box had already been opened, and there was no closing it. I was a very inquisitive and deep-thinking child; the subject of my lost twin became something that I was compelled to explore. Truth be told, I was fascinated by it. How were we all alive in this world when the other half of me is missing? Where do you go when you die? What do the gates of heaven look like? Were there actually gates? Why was it my twin who was lost and not me? Was my twin someone now looking over me and protecting me? Had I lost a twin brother or sister?

I looked at my twin brothers Jason and Wayne and understood just how close such siblings can be. From that moment on, my lost twin effectively became my youthful concept of a guardian angel. Over time, I came to believe that I was somehow living a life for both of us. But I also came to understand the fragility of life – that the absolute certainty of life I understood as a child wasn't quite the reality of the world we lived in.

In a way, to use a *Harry Potter* metaphor, it was as if the cloak of invisibility had dropped from my shoulders and suddenly I was exposed to the harsh reality of what life can involve – loss, heartache, unfairness and danger. These were concepts I had never before known. Perhaps another child would have simply pushed them aside and moved on with their happy, carefree life. But I wasn't the type to shrug my shoulders, ignore something and merrily go on my way. I wanted to know the who, what, why, where, when and how. That's the type of person I was.

Despite being 12, I suddenly understood the stark reality of the loss my mother had suffered. I thought about that little person inside my mother's tummy, and then the fact that they were suddenly and inexplicably gone – and, as far as I could understand at the time, gone without a reason. She must have been devastated. I also thought about my place in the world without the other half of me.

When I look back at that garden incident and paint a picture of my life before that day, it was in vivid colours. Afterwards, there was a seeping grey around the edges. I was confused and had no outlet to resolve these feelings. It was apparent my mother didn't want to speak about it again – and I knew she only wanted to protect me. Despite my years, I was also canny enough to understand that the subject should not be broached again.

Yet as children we need to express ourselves, to speak and be listened to, and our worries to be addressed and not ignored. I know that my mother was doing what she believed to be best for me, but today I really wish she had spoken to me – even in terms that were broad and general. It wasn't even so much the issue of the twin. I think it was more the fact that I didn't get to normalise or process it. I didn't have somebody to confide in, to share my secret. I couldn't Google anything at the time. If there was counselling available, I had never heard of it in our community.

At that time, if you had a problem, you went or were brought to the parish priest. If you wanted to see the priest, it felt like making an appointment with God! They were essentially all-powerful within the community. But I just didn't feel it was something I could bring up with a priest – most likely because I was afraid it would then be referred straight back to my mother, who had already clearly ruled on the matter.

I am sure, now, that the loss of my twin wouldn't have had such an impact on me if I had had an outlet to talk about it. Everyone dies. It's a part of life. But to become aware of this, we need to be given the freedom to ask questions. We don't do children any favours when we try to shield them from answers that they are seeking honestly at an age when it can be explained to them in straightforward terms.

Ancient cultures believed that a twin who was safely born after losing a twin in pregnancy had a special connection, almost a subconscious link to another dimension. I often wondered, was the other half of me out there somewhere? In some ancient religions, a so-called 'twinless twin' was even believed to have unique powers of perception, particularly when it came to emotions and loss. Some cultures used such 'twinless twins' as oracles or seers in special ceremonies.

In today's world, the unique aspect of loss involved in being a 'twinless twin' has led to various support groups and associations, including the Twinless Twins Support Group International. I was shocked to discover how many people there are just like myself, including some very famous celebrities who have lost twins. These include actors David Jason and Sophie Turner, musicians Elvis Presley and Liberace, as well as Jay Kay of Jamiroquai.

Certain tribes in Africa associated twins with the spirit world, with some Nigerian tribes considering twins to be a special kind of 'spirit children'. The Yoruba believed that twins had an especially close connection to the supernatural and could bring either great blessings or great suffering to their families and tribe. The Yoruba were particularly concerned if one twin should die – particularly before or during childbirth. In these cases, a special statuette was commissioned by the best artist in the tribe, to honour the 'lost twin'. These statuettes came to be known as Ere Ibeji statues, and are today among the most valuable pieces of ancient African art.

I was fascinated to discover that among the Yoruba the rate of twin births was extraordinarily high. Sadly, before the advent of modern medicine, the infant mortality rate was equally as high. In the early nineteenth century, one British explorer, Richard Lander, was astounded to discover Yoruba mothers carrying a healthy child alongside a carved Ere Ibeji statue.

Baffled by what was going on, he later realised that the statue was to honour or commemorate a lost twin. In Yoruba tradition, twins are believed to be the children of Shango, the god of thunder and lightning, one of their most powerful deities. They are also thought to possess supernatural powers and share the same soul. The Ere Ibeji statue was, in essence, a way of helping the mother and tribe to cope with the grief of losing a twin. They believed that the intricately carved statuette would honour the deceased twin – and serve as a receptacle for half of the shared soul.

The mother of the departed twin carried the Ere Ibeji tucked in her baby wrapper and treated it as a live infant in the belief that to deny twins was to invite their wrath. The statue was treated as if it were alive – and given an honoured role in all tribal ceremonies.

Perhaps my mother sharing my twin's fate with me that day helped her to come to terms? I hope so.

While I was fascinated by how ancient cultures accorded great importance to twins, I don't believe I have any special insight into other dimensions or the supernatural. But I was taken by how cultures felt it vitally important to support mothers and families in their grief at the loss of a twin. Not only that, but how cultures believed that a twin who had lost a sibling was somehow specially sensitive to loss, or had a deeper connection to the emotions surrounding grief than other individuals.

Over my life, I have certainly felt things very deeply. I have always felt the need to explore and understand all the elements of my pain and happiness in equal measure. To be honest, it is not a choice – I feel compelled to do it. Even today, that need is something I don't fully understand.

Years later, I wondered whether my discovery of my lost twin was somehow to prepare me for the trials and tribulations that lay ahead.

In July 1988 I got a job in a local aluminium factory in Limerick. I finished Sixth Year in school and began working full time at the factory as a general operative. It was a great time – the people I worked alongside were the salt of the earth, I had a reasonable income and there was a great social scene in Limerick.

I met my husband, Dave, in August 1989 and we began dating. We made a great couple – I instantly felt safe and comfortable with him, almost as if we were pieces of a jigsaw that were somehow destined to be together. With Dave, I felt secure, happy and content. Together, we made a formidable team, each bringing out the very best in the other and always being one another's biggest champion.

I was 18 years old when I got pregnant. I was head over heels in love with Dave, and marriage was something we both wanted. But getting pregnant so young certainly changed the early years we had planned together in economic terms.

It was a cold November morning in 1990 when I discovered I was pregnant. Dave and I both worked in the same factory. He accompanied me to the family planning centre that day and waited for me, seated on a park bench, as I went inside. That's the kind of supportive man he is. They told us the test would take an hour, so we walked around Limerick to pass the time.

Back at the centre, I froze as the assistant told me the test had been positive, and that I was pregnant. My son Dean – who was born on 22 April 1991 – is one of the great blessings of my life. But back on that day of fear and worry my first reaction to the news was utter devastation. I was a truly terrified teenager.

My mind went into overdrive with questions I didn't have answers to. What would my mother say? What would the neighbours think? How did I get myself here? Would Dave want a future with me and our soon-to-be-born baby? How would we manage financially?

Now, I look back and smile. Not everyone was judging me, and the overwhelming majority of my family and friends were hugely supportive.

But there were funny moments. At one point I didn't know if the knot in my stomach was nerves or the result of morning sickness. But, even then, I gravitated towards the place where I wanted to be, the master of my own destiny.

We had to live in a rented flat, which was, to put it mildly, in need of substantial refurbishment. It was damp and cold, and the roof leaked. Dean had asthma as a baby, and the conditions in our flat resulted in us having to take him to the emergency department on multiple occasions. Dave and I dreamed of owning our own home, but that would be in the future, despite our focus on saving every penny we possibly could.

It was scary for us both in the early years. We were barely adults ourselves, and yet here we were trying to be good parents. But I was blessed to have met a good, kind and decent man – someone I could build a life with. Like my parents, in the early years we didn't have a lot of money, but we were committed as life partners.

Whatever my parents might have wanted, there wasn't the financial wherewithal to send me to university, particularly after my father was made redundant from his job. Plus, I now had a baby to look after. So, a few years after Dean was born, I signed up for night school at Limerick Institute of Technology (LIT), even though, after my maternity leave, I resumed my work at the factory. We just couldn't afford for me not to return to work.

Two nights each week I went to LIT for night courses. It was hard trying to juggle work, home life and study, but I knew education was the key to a better future for all of us. As I got older, the value of education and training became ever more apparent to me – a conviction I shared with my brother Jason.

I wanted to work, to better myself. Not just for my own sake but to set an example for my children. And after almost four years of saving, Dave and I had a sufficient deposit to secure a mortgage and buy a house. We signed the papers in 1993 and finally had our first home. Jason moved in with us and helped us with babysitting and covering running costs for the property.

On 18 August 1994 Dave and I married, and it was the happiest day of my life. We weren't just husband and wife – we were best friends and comrades in the great adventure of life. Together we were forging the life we had dreamed of, both for ourselves and for our children.

In 1995 my hard work and commitment to education and up-skilling began to pay off as I was promoted into a management position at the factory where I worked. It was a source of enormous pride to me that I was the first woman to be promoted into a management position at the factory, which employed over 250 staff.

On 21 March 2001, our second son, Adam, was born. During my maternity leave, I became more ambitious for myself career-wise and, having proven myself in a management role, began to consider other, more highly paid roles. Just five months after Adam was born I secured the position of quality controller with an insulation company based in Askeaton. The salary was much more attractive than what I had been receiving, and it helped enormously with our family finances.

Within 18 months I was promoted again – now I was responsible for quality control at all plants manufacturing insulation products within the umbrella parent company. It was a position with a great deal of responsibility, and securing the prestigious ISO 9001 quality standard for the plants fell to me.

Financially, we were in a much stronger position, and Dave and I decided to upgrade our home by purchasing a series of larger houses in need of renovation, living in them while refurbishing them, and then eventually selling them on. It was a time of rising property values in Ireland, and we benefited accordingly.

It was hard work. Dave and I would work all day, spend family time with the children in the evening and then at night and at weekends try to tackle the refurbishment jobs needed in the house.

Eventually, I got a job with a not-for-profit organisation working to help support the socioeconomic development of Limerick. Dave had passed an advertisement to me in 2009 for the position of enterprise manager at the centre, and I had been intrigued, even though it represented a total change from my previous roles.

Until that point, I had been a senior manager in major manufacturing companies. But I had numerous bosses to answer to above me. The role Dave showed me at Southill would involve me running my own show and being focused on the community sector. What intrigued me was the idea of working in the voluntary sector and making a contribution to my own community. If I did my job well, everyone in the community benefited – and I thought that was the best reward you could possibly have.

I didn't have a Master's or a PhD, but I had a doctorate in life experience and hard work. Eventually, I became chief executive at the not-for-profit. When I joined it had just been forced to make staff redundant. It was a challenging environment for a fledgling chief executive, to put it mildly.

But I relished the challenge. Essentially, my job was to focus on social enterprise; I built funding models that allowed for the delivery of deep retrofits for fuel-poor homes in Limerick city and county.

I worked 60 to 80 hours a week and was relentless in my goal of easing poverty in the most socioeconomically deprived areas we were responsible for. Over time we expanded, and I was very proud that 90 per cent of our staff were drawn from local employment activation programmes. Eventually, we expanded to the point where we had 160 staff and played a role in the transformation of large swathes of Limerick society.

In ways, our work was like a drop in the ocean in tackling social disadvantage. But we made a big difference at a local level – we helped people improve their homes, we encouraged education initiatives, we promoted employment schemes and staunchly backed people who wanted to enhance their community through their own business ventures, whether it was a café, a crèche, a community grocery or a beauty salon.

One of the projects I was most proud of was the Team Limerick Clean-Up, where people from all backgrounds and social groups were brought together and helped enhance the environment of their own community and, in the process, built pride in where they lived. I learned a crucial life lesson – that, in giving, it is often the person who gives rather than the person who receives who has the greatest reward.

Dave and I had also been considering fostering children, something we had been interested in for some time. In ways, it was another reflection of the work we were committed to. It also represented a commitment by both of us to try to share our good fortune in life with a child who was less fortunate, and who needed a safe, loving environment.

We both underwent special training courses in 2013 and, in 2015, fostered our first little girl. Words fail me to describe the happiness that the 13-year-old brought to our lives in such a short space of time – she was feisty and funny, and soon our entire family doted on her. Even though she was only with us for a couple of months, I felt we had helped show her what a difference a happy family environment can make.

My time with the not-for-profit ended – as you will read later – for family reasons in late 2019, and I formally left in January 2020, leaving behind more than a decade of fond memories. Later, I served as manager of a mental health group in the midwest, a role I was very proud of, even though it proved to be far shorter than I had originally anticipated.

Those jobs taught me the value of trusting my own instincts when it came to people and work. I saw at first hand how some people put the project and the team before themselves – to deliver without fuss on every single task assigned to them. Such people are a joy and an inspiration to work alongside. Then there were others who wanted all the credit, who loved the sound of their own voices and whose apparent talent was for doing nothing while making themselves look overworked.

Over time, I fine-tuned my ability to assess the people I worked with. I dealt with everyone from the poorest of the poor to some of the wealthiest people in Ireland, from people who couldn't read and were third-generation unemployed to individuals who could speak multiple languages and had several university degrees.

I discovered that, when I formed a good first impression of someone, it was rarely misleading. Likewise, when I met my brother Jason's beautiful new girlfriend, Margaret 'Mags' Fitzpatrick, I immediately liked her. There seemed to be an aura around Mags – a sense of honesty, kindness and loyalty. I felt drawn to Mags, and knew, almost without doubt, that she would be good for my brother.

They were only dating a short time when I came to consider Mags as a good friend. By the time Jason and Mags got married in 2003, I regarded her almost like a younger sister. Dave already considered Jason as a brother, and it was no surprise that we spent a lot of our time with them as a couple. They would look after our children when we went on 'date nights', and they sought our advice about everything from building their dream home to finances and savings.

The friends of my brothers, Wayne and Jason, also largely became friends of Dave and myself. They were my brothers' friends, but I felt comfortable around them. It is hardly surprising that they would become some of the closest pals of Dave and myself over the years. In the difficult days that lay ahead, they would prove their friendship over and over again.

In contrast, I have met people either socially or through work who I instantly became wary of – almost as if a 'red flag' has been raised at a subconscious level about them. It is difficult to explain, but it was as if an inner voice was warning me to be careful and not too trusting, mindful that some people are not as they seem. I can't explain how or why, but it is just an inner feeling of wariness I get around some people. My intuition would guide me, and I listened. I would devise a list – one I called the 'red list' – of people whom I couldn't avoid but needed to manage my time around and interactions with.

For the most part, these inner warnings have proven to be unerringly accurate with individuals attempting to take advantage of our family either through business dealings, personal contacts or even the tortuous process of campaigning for justice for my murdered brother, Jason.

I have no idea whether these inner feelings or heightened perceptions are in any way linked to my 'lost twin'. Probably not. But what I do know is that I ignored such deep inner concerns once to the eternal regret of both myself and my family. I live with that knowledge every single day.

REMINDER

True friends are more precious than gold, silver or platinum. They are the people who are there for us through thick and thin.

2

THE TOLL OF HEARTBREAK

believe there is a link between grief and the unfairness we perceive in life. The impact of a death on us can be influenced by a vast set of circumstances that can make it all the harder and more painful to bear – the circumstances of the person's passing, their age, their legacy and the timing of their death.

We are heartbroken if a person in their 80s who we love dearly passes away. But our grief is, almost subconsciously, quelled by their age, the wonderful life they enjoyed, the role they played in our lives – and if they had been in pain from an illness, perhaps we see their passing as offering them relief from suffering. If the legacy they leave behind involves children, grandchildren, great-grandchildren and a lifetime of great memories, it can shape the nature of our grief.

Sometimes a death that occurs at Christmas or another festive time is harder to grieve, because of the conflicting memories we face in having to cope with it – we're delighted with the happiness associated with Christmas but constantly reminded of the loved one no longer with us. It is almost as if the festive occasion clashes with our grief, making us feel guilty for having any happiness at such a time of year. It creates a juxtaposition between love and grief, life and death.

I am not for one minute suggesting that there is some kind of formula for sadness and loss, but when a person dies long before their time, it makes the grief harder to bear, makes it harder to come to terms with the loss and to cope with its consequences. When that person dies needlessly or is the victim of a violent crime, the loss is increased beyond comprehension. In those circumstances, how can you make sense of the senseless? The unfairness surges to the surface, and you are left bereft, adrift with only negative emotions such as sadness, anger and despair to grab hold of.

I know because I have been that person struggling in a sea of pain, frustrated to the point of making poor decisions and indulging in precisely the wrong type of behaviour and emotions for myself and my family. Let me explain why.

Jason was besotted with Mags from the very moment he set eyes on her. Their love was one of reciprocated affection, total commitment, shared passion and common life goals. They had the same aims and they adored each other, and we all fully expected them to grow old together.

They were 'that' couple – you know, the one you envy, as they were just so damned nice. She was beautiful inside and out, had unique features and was so darn funny, sometimes when she didn't intend to be. She loved a strong cup of tea and a good natter, the very same as a good night out on the town. Mags was a girl's girl.

Neither Jason nor Mags gave two hoots about showing their affection for each other in public. They had a shared vision for life that emulated mine and Dave's. We base our relationship on friendship, respect and common life goals. We didn't come from backgrounds that had the rite of passage to third-level education, or parents who could help us financially, so we aspired to work hard, grow our careers and earn everything we got.

We were young, laughed a lot and felt invincible. We were hopeful, excited about future opportunities and not afraid to work hard for them. I can hear a whisper of Mags's laughter as I write this. In my mind's eye, I can see that furtive look that Mags and Jason often shared, as if they could communicate through only a glance. They operated on such a deep level that sometimes they didn't need words.

Jason had grown up to be a handsome, confident man, blessed with a wonderful personality, a sense of humour and a fine singing voice. He had an appetite for hard work and was determined to get on in life. He didn't have the advantage of a third-level education, but he embraced every opportunity in life to enhance his skill set and become more valuable to his employers. Life had been generous in bestowing its gifts on Jason.

I think it is a measure of the type of person my brother was that he entered the firm he worked for on the factory floor as a general operative. He worked hard, moved up the promotions ladder, undertook night classes and eventually ended up running an entire plant in North Carolina as a senior executive for the same firm.

In Irish terms at least, Jason was blessed. Never shy around the fairer sex, Jason had a succession of stunning girlfriends, several of whom I would also go on to consider friends. In fact, Jason remained friends with all of his ex-girlfriends after they broke up, which I think reflects the type of kind and respectful man he was.

Jason celebrated his 21st birthday party at the Sally Port in Limerick in February 1997 in a joint party with his twin brother, Wayne. It was a very popular venue in Limerick at the time, and the place was packed with family and friends for what turned out to be a great night. One of Jason's old friends from Our Lady Queen of Peace primary school, Lynn Shanahan, made a surprise appearance. The two had known each other since they were four years old. Jason and herself caught up on old times and resumed their friendship.

Both were at a party later that year when Jason nonchalantly asked his friend Lynn about the beautiful girl at the party, who worked with Lynn at the crèche. It was Mags. After the party, when Mags suggested cooking up a full Irish breakfast for the remaining partygoers, it was Jason who walked her to the shop to buy groceries. Before the house emptied that day, Jason and Mags were holding hands and making plans for their first date.

Mags was slender and had beautiful hazel eyes and dark hair that perfectly framed her pretty face. She was careful with her appearance and had a natural sense of style. But Mags's good looks paled in comparison with her inner beauty. She was soft-spoken, kind and generous. The young woman I got to know spent much of her time thinking of others – her family, friends, workmates and, of course, Jason.

There was a subtle elegance about her that struck everyone who met her. Mags wasn't one of those women who make a striking entrance into a room and then, having grabbed attention, had very little to say for herself. Her looks never changed the kindness inherent in her personality. She was interested in other people, loved conversation and was deeply loyal to her friends. Above all, it was clear that her life revolved around her family – and that impressed everyone in our family who cherished the same values.

It wasn't long before I knew my brother was smitten with this beautiful, striking woman. He never forgot a birthday or special occasion – even remembering presents for her on the anniversary of their first date. Jason regularly arranged flowers to be delivered to Mags's workplace. She would pretend to be annoyed at the cost of the flowers but was privately delighted at the loving gesture from her boyfriend.

Mags fitted seamlessly into our family. She joined us for holidays in County Clare, and became a favourite of our son, Dean, who was then only five. Dean loved nothing better than when his mother and father went out for a meal and left him with Jason and Mags as babysitters. Mags selflessly gave time to Dean, chatting or playing with colouring books with him. It was the same when our second son, Adam, arrived.

It wasn't long before the relationship moved onto a serious footing. I was very close to Jason, and I knew he was captivated by Mags. He had lived with us for a time when he was working, and I knew he wanted the type of relationship Dave and I were fortunate to share. On occasions when Jason would go out to play golf with Dave and his friends, Mags would join me and my friends for girls-only breaks. On one trip to London, she delayed the whole plane as the clip on her safety belt wouldn't lock. The flight was full, so we couldn't move seats. It was only resolved when the pilot came down to help. We laughed the whole way to the hotel in London.

On other occasions, we would all head off together for short city breaks – often to coincide with rugby matches our beloved Munster were playing in England, Scotland or France. It was a golden time. For an all-too-brief period, it felt like we had it all. Some of my most cherished memories today are of those trips – the happiness we shared, the sheer joy we all took in each other's company and how unaware we all were of the unpredictable cruelties of life.

Jason surprised no one when he proposed to Mags while on holiday in Barcelona in 2002. My brother had carefully done his research, and he asked Mags to marry him at the stunning Montjuïc fountain. It was a beautifully romantic engagement setting.

Mags was beaming when they arrived back from Spain, and proudly showed us the ring. It was as if she was aglow with an inner light. Their wedding in 2003 was like something from a fairy tale. They married at the Star of the Sea Church in Quilty, County Clare – Mags and our family loved Clare – and they chose to have both the ceremony and the subsequent reception there.

The reception was hosted at the Bellbridge House Hotel in nearby Miltown Malbay. It was a fitting venue, because so many of our childhood memories were associated with the hotel when it operated as just a bed and breakfast. The incredible Clare coastal countryside formed the backdrop of their wedding photographs, and I still have copies of those glorious images in my sitting room today. If you look at these photos in our home, the background remains the same, but the people in the images are fading as the years progress. It is a strong symbolism, one shared by many homes all over the world as we deal with loss and grief.

The wedding brought out Jason's romantic side. He had written a series of special notes for Mags, which she was instructed to open in sequence before their wedding day. On the evening before the wedding, Mags's father, Michael, found his daughter weeping in the bathroom of their family home and presumed she wanted to call the wedding off. Instead, Mags had just read one of Jason's notes and was overcome with emotion at the devotion of the man who was about to become her husband and soulmate.

Their first child, Jack, was born in September 2004. In September 2006, Mags gave birth to their second child, Sarah. I thought Jason's heart would burst with pride. His perfect family was now complete – and he loved nothing better than having us visit in the dream home he had built on the outskirts of Limerick city.

It was heart-warming to watch how animated Jason and Mags became when they were talking about their new home – the landscaping they planned, the colours for the various rooms, the type of furniture they wanted, the children's bedrooms. Today, when I close my eyes and remember those halcyon days, I recall them as a picture-perfect image of pure happiness. Then everything changed.

The awful events of 21 November 2006 are scorched onto my memory, and introduced me to a grief that I never before imagined existed in this world. Just over 12 weeks after Sarah's birth, Mags died.

It began as the kind of evening we had shared so many times before. Jason, Mags, Dave and myself had chatted on the phone in the early evening. Later that night, Dave and I prepared for bed in our Raheen home. Indeed, at first, all was calm and normal in both homes. Mags's sister, Catherine, was staying with Jason and Mags at their new home as she saved for her own home. All had seemed well; Mags had joked with Jason and her sister about the dishwasher being unemptied. She fed the children and went to bed. Around midnight, she fed Sarah and briefly chatted with Jason before falling back to sleep. Just over an hour later, Mags woke Jason to say she was having an asthma attack.

Mags had had asthma attacks before and had even had to be treated in hospital. None of the attacks had been that severe, but it was a condition she kept a close eye on nonetheless. Jason had insisted that Mags always have her nebuliser close at hand in the house, and that night Mags immediately began using the nebuliser but, for some reason, it failed to offer her any relief. Her chest pains were getting worse rather than better, and she was struggling to breathe.

Jason woke Catherine to tell her what was happening. Catherine went to check on her sister and Mags admitted to her that she was frightened by the unrelenting nature of her asthma attack. Jason called for an ambulance and Catherine did her best to comfort her sister.

By now, Mags was terrified. She kept repeating to her sister, 'I'm going to die, I'm going to die.' Catherine and Jason reassured her that everything would be alright, and that help was on the way. But Jason knew that the ambulance would take some time to reach the house, and so he decided to cut the response time by driving to meet the paramedics.

Catherine later recalled that she knew the situation was critical when she watched her sister be carried to Jason's car in her pyjamas – Mags never left the house unless her clothing, hair and make-up were perfect. The car sped off with Catherine left to care for little Jack and Sarah.

Jason sped towards the agreed meeting point for the ambulance, but it hadn't arrived. As they pulled over to the meeting point, Mags suddenly slumped forward in her seat. Panicked, Jason remembered his workplace medical training and commenced cardiopulmonary resuscitation on his wife. He desperately kept doing CPR, and finally Mags was revived. A few minutes later the paramedics arrived and took over care of Mags. It was only a few minutes between Mags slumping forward in the car and the paramedics arriving, but I imagine they were the most terrifying of my brother's life.

The ambulance rushed her to University Hospital Limerick (UHL), where emergency department doctors battled to help her. Jason had followed the ambulance in his car and, after parking it at UHL, ran to the emergency department. But Mags had stopped breathing in the ambulance on the way to the hospital, and the paramedics were unable to revive her. When they arrived at the hospital, it was too late for doctors to successfully intervene. As Jason stood alone in the emergency room, a doctor informed him that his wife, the love of his life, had been pronounced dead.

The UHL team had also contacted Dave and myself. We were both asleep in bed when the phone rang. Startled, I looked at Dave as he answered the phone – and instantly knew something was wrong from the look on his face. The call was from a nurse at the UHL emergency department. She said Mags was in a serious condition and advised us to get there as quickly as we could, because Jason needed us.

The hospital is only a two-minute drive from our Raheen home, and we were there within minutes. Jason was disconsolate. I felt utterly useless, and wept as I saw my brother holding his dead wife's hand and begging her through his tears not to leave him and their children. At one point, Jason stood up and stared at the ceiling with his eyes closed – almost as if he wanted to scream in agony to the heavens above at the unfairness of it.

I just couldn't comprehend the scene. Mags looked so peaceful. She was wearing a beautiful blue and white pyjama set and, at first glance, appeared to be gently sleeping. She looked tiny on the hospital gurney. Her eyes were closed and her delicate, stunning features were almost serene. Her peacefulness seemed totally at odds with the scene around her: the cardiac monitoring equipment, the oxygen bottles, the tubes, all the trappings of a hospital emergency department.

I was in shock because we had no inkling of the attack. Mags had been tired, but she had only given birth to Sarah some 12 weeks before. She had had the flu several weeks before, but only had mild symptoms, and quickly made a good recovery. After Mags had given birth to Sarah, both families went to Spanish Point to spend a few weeks relaxing and helping out as we enjoyed the new addition to our family. The boys would do nine holes of golf as we made breakfast, and when they passed the back door of the house we would call out that it was ready. We would tuck Adam and Jack into bed at night after they gave Sarah a kiss and a squeeze, and they would be so worn out from the beach that they would be asleep in minutes. We would head to the sunroom, with Mags or I holding Sarah as we chatted and watched the sun set.

Mags loved nothing better than organising parties and family celebrations. Just five weeks before, she had organised a wonderful second birthday party for Jack. Two weeks before her death, we celebrated Sarah's christening, which was something she had eagerly looked forward to, and she had thrown herself into every detail of the event. Now we were in an emergency room, and it felt as though someone had thrown a bomb into all our lives.

We used to joke that Mags and Jason had it all – good looks, a dream home, decent incomes from two excellent jobs, a fairy-tale love affair and the perfect family with two beautiful, healthy children. In an instant, it was snatched away.

Jason was bereft, and looked at Dave and me through tear-stained eyes. I knew my brother was praying that this was all a nightmare, that all he had to do was to wake up to banish the pain. All we could do was shed our own tears with him. Eventually, he pulled himself together enough to remember Mags's sister Catherine, who was back at their home looking after Jack and Sarah. Jason got his mobile phone and rang Catherine to murmur the painful words: 'She's gone.'

Within minutes, Jason's tight circle of friends began to arrive at UHL. They comforted Jason, tried to help with some of the arrangements and made the phone calls that spared Jason further agony. The doctors were incredibly kind. Later, we would learn that Mags had, as we had feared, suffered a major asthma attack. Unlike her previous attacks, this one had exerted tremendous strain on her heart, which had simply stopped beating.

A retired GP and friend of the family later explained to us what had happened based on the post-mortem findings. Mags had suffered what was referred to as status asthmaticus – a form of respiratory failure that occurs from the worst form of acute, severe asthma. Such is the severity of the asthma attack that it is usually not responsive to normal treatments. The only option is urgent ventilation. However, it can be so severe that even hospital patients with ready access to ventilation have succumbed to it. In Mags's case, her system was unable to cope with the low levels of oxygen. It was nothing short of a miracle that Jason was able to revive her by the roadside.

Mags had so much to live for – a husband who adored her, two gorgeous children she had just brought into the world and a dream home they had only recently moved into. But despite her burning desire to live, it just wasn't enough. A woman with such vast space in her heart for others found it just wasn't strong enough to keep beating for herself.

I want to be clear, there is no way on this earth that Mags would have chosen to leave, to die. If love could have saved her, she would be alive right now. But we just don't get to choose, and no one is exempt.

The following days were a haze of pain and bewilderment. Jason was devastated. My big-hearted brother wasn't able to pay his own tribute to Mags at the Requiem Mass. He was simply too devastated.

Dave agreed to deliver the final farewell on Jason's behalf, in words carefully written by my brother over the previous 48 hours.

It read: 'To my soul mate and beautiful wife, Mag Mag … don't worry about the babies. All of us here today, family and friends, will make sure that they always remember how great their Mommy was. I promise I will stay strong for our wonderful kids. The love and warmth and offers of support we have received from everyone makes me so proud of the person you are. You always said that I was lucky to have you – you were the girl of my dreams and then became the love of my life. Now you are the girl of my dreams again. My Mag Mag. I'll love you all of my life. Please look in on us from time to time. Love you always and forever. Jason.'

Jack was just two years and two months old. Sarah was only 12 weeks old. Jason was 30 years old and now a widower. He had built the house on the outskirts of Limerick as the home that Mags had always wanted. Her photographs were on mantelpieces, walls and tables throughout the home. Every time I went to visit, the wall colourings and furnishings reminded me of Mags. Every time a door opened, I half expected her to pop her head around and ask Jason why the kettle wasn't on for tea.

Initially, Jason buried himself in caring for his children. They became his life. In truth, they were tangible links to his lost love, and I think my brother looked at them and saw Mags. Just weeks after his wife's death, he brought Jack and Sarah to see Santa Claus as part of a workplace family event – and the photo of that festive season moment still brings tears to my eyes. It was hard to witness such raw grief, to watch him struggle with two buggies, nappy bags, changes of baby clothes, bottles and teething. Grief did not stop the practicalities of having two babies to care for.

Jason's family and friends rallied to help him. He was

swamped with offers of help, from babysitting to house-cleaning and from hot meals to washing. Mags's sister, Catherine, was a stalwart support, as were Mags's friends Lynn and Karen, as well as our sister, Marilyn. We would help look after Jack and Sarah alongside our own boys, Dean and Adam. Jason's employers were incredible to him, and he was given time to get things sorted to enable him to return to work. Everyone tried to help, but ultimately Jason had to work through the terrible loss on his own – we couldn't help him with that unless we were invited to do so.

It was a dark November and December. Jason came to stay with Dave, myself, Dean and Adam. We tried to make it as festive a Christmas as possible for Jack and Sarah. Mercifully, they were both too young to fully comprehend what had just happened. All they understood was that they wanted their mammy – and when they called out for her in vain it was like a dagger being twisted in my heart. When Jack would turn to me and ask for his mammy, all I could do was cuddle him and hold him close.

It was Dave's mother who provided the stimulus to help us get through. A woman full of spirit, she was blessed with a sunny demeanour and a wonderful sense of humour. She worked overtime to try to bring a little cheer to us all. It may have been a wasted effort by her at the time, but it gave us just enough light to get through that awful Christmas.

There were days it was hard. I realised that Jason was

driving to Castlemungret Cemetery on his lunch break, just to be near Mags. I learned he would stand by the graveside and talk aloud to her. On other occasions he would read aloud from the local paper, filling her in on all the Limerick news and gossip. Sometimes he would just eat his lunch and stare at the headstone.

On Christmas, St Valentine's Day, her birthday, their wedding anniversary and the anniversary of their first date, Jason would travel to Mags's grave to read aloud the card he had chosen and his handwritten verse to her. Jason would then bring the cards and letters back home and carefully store them in a drawer. He wanted all the memories of his wife to be kept safe for Jack and Sarah in the future.

His moments of welcome relief came from the children. Jason's world revolved around them – when he wasn't working, he was with the children. He particularly loved taking them to Clare, which he now associated with Mags as much as he did with his own childhood. Sarah's first steps were an incredible source of happiness for him, as was Jack's first day at playschool.

We were all delighted to maintain the support network around Jason – Dave and I adored having Jack and Sarah spend time at our home, while Catherine and Marilyn loved the children as if they were their own – but I think my brother slowly became determined to try to work out independent arrangements. I suspect Jason realised his recovery from grief hinged on him easing back a little on the support from family and friends and slowly finding his own feet and a daily regime that worked for him.

His first step was to hire an au pair. This would give him support in the family home and ease his reliance on family and friends for childminding while he was at work. It was a great idea, but it didn't work out as Jason hoped. He had two au pairs, Spanish and Czech girls, over a nine-month period. Both were lovely girls, quite friendly and very good with Jack and Sarah. But the arrangements didn't work out to suit either party. Both girls had only limited English, which, unfortunately, became a complicating factor in the care arrangements. Another issue was that Jason lived outside Limerick in a beautiful country area. But, for a young foreign au pair, it was a little isolated, particularly when Jason was at work.

While Jason wanted a medium-term arrangement for Jack and Sarah, the two girls were only interested in short-term contracts. Jason wanted stability for the two children – he didn't want a succession of au pairs for the children to have to get used to and then, when they were familiar with them, suddenly have them leave with all the turmoil that would cause. He wanted a more stable arrangement.

Friends felt Jason opting for an au pair was a positive step; it showed he was trying to re-establish independence in his life from reliance on his family and friends. Some friends saw it as the first step in dealing with grief and undertaking his path to recovery.

Tragically, the next au pair introduced to our lives was Molly Martens, a young American woman who at first appeared to be the answer to Jason's prayers. Little did we suspect at the time that she would become a creature to haunt our very worst nightmares.

Molly, who was from Tennessee, was scouring advertisements for nannies both in the US and in English-speaking countries. We had no inkling at the time, but she had no experience of being a nanny, had a history of mental health problems and, we realised far too late, had somehow come to believe that children offered a pathway to escape from her problems in life.

She was a drop-out from a prestigious US college and had drifted between a series of low-paid jobs. Molly was now 25, and apparently adrift in life. Her family, who had connections to a series of top US colleges and mostly worked for the federal government, never spoke openly about Molly's mental health struggles.

In years that followed, speaking to Molly was like dealing with a Walter Mitty-like character – the stories were fascinating, but you never quite knew where the truth stopped and fiction began. In fact, within our family, it became a standing joke that when someone said something far-fetched they were told: 'You sound like Molly now!'

Only a few weeks after being released from a mental health clinic in late 2007, Molly apparently hit on the idea of going overseas to care for children. The adverts she focused on involved widowed men with young children. She was particularly interested in looking after young girls. Jason's advertisement seemed to fit the bill perfectly given his age and the tender years of his two children. She made direct contact with my brother.

Molly arrived in Ireland from Boston with a one-way ticket in March 2008. Irish immigration authorities were immediately suspicious of her, with no return ticket and no fixed work arrangements in Ireland. She was promptly put on the next plane back to the US. Tragically, as it would prove, Molly managed to make contact with Jason (who was waiting at Shannon Airport to collect her) and made arrangements to travel back to Ireland in 24 hours, this time via Dublin.

Jason's friend Lynn was also at the airport that day, and immediately felt this young American woman was entirely wrong for Jason's situation. Lynn bluntly said she was the last thing Jason needed in his life. I didn't meet Molly until later that month, as we were away on holidays. My inner voice was somehow urging caution but, truth be told, I liked Molly at that first meeting, and didn't heed my gut instinct. She seemed friendly and warm, and there was no doubting her commitment to care for Jack and Sarah. My hospitable Irish instincts took over, and I was determined to try to help a young woman far from home feel happy and comfortable in Ireland.

We were all misled. Molly wasn't what she seemed; her history of childminding was entirely fabricated, and by the time we realised that much of her personal story was a total fantasy, it was too late. Jason had commenced a relationship with her and, within a few months, it was moving at a pace that alarmed both his family and his friends.

I tried to urge caution, to slow the pace of the relationship while also trying to carefully negotiate the minefield of minding my own business in my brother's life. I know my brother's friends also gently tried to advise him to take things easy. Jason himself tried to apply the brakes with the relationship but, in a short space of time, it was Jason's broken heart that was dictating matters, rather than his head.

None of us knew until it was too late, but Molly was waging a relentless campaign to put the relationship on a firm, permanent footing, to persuade Jason to sell his dream home built for Mags – Molly said she felt as if she was constantly in Mags's shadow in the house – and, finally, to relocate from Ireland to the US.

If Jason was on his own, perhaps things might have been different. Maybe he would have ended the relationship with Molly during one of her bouts of personal demands. But shortly after Molly began caring for the children, little Sarah began referring to her as 'Mammy'. We didn't know it, but

Molly privately encouraged the little girl to use this title with her. She surrounded Sarah with books, which she read to her every night, called *Mommy and Me*, *Sunny Days with Mommy & Me* and *Mommy and Me – How I Came to Be*. In years to come, Molly would get furious with Jack when he would refuse to call her his mother. We had absolutely no idea what was going on.

Molly began dressing Sarah and herself in similar outfits. She seemed happiest when she was alone with the children and, during family gatherings, would often drift away from adult company to spend time alone with Jack and Sarah. Over time, I also became curious about the fact that none of Molly's American friends ever came to visit her.

For his part, Jason was bombarded with pleas from Molly – both written and verbal – for him not to turn his back on love. In one email I discovered after Jason's death, Molly had warned him not to reject love when life had given him a second chance at giving his heart to someone. None of us realised it, but she was manipulating a vulnerable, wounded father, and knew precisely which buttons to press. She was now acting like the de facto mother of his two children, and Jason once confided in me that he couldn't bear the thought of taking a second mother-figure away from his children and dealing with all the upset that would cause.

In hindsight, I struggle to understand how we were all so comprehensively misled. I looked at my brother and I saw that the terrible burden of grief imposed on him by Mags's death had been eased. With relief, I noted he was smiling and laughing like he did before that terrible November 2006 evening. At the time, I was willing to overlook Molly's flights of fantasy and her bizarre behaviour if her involvement in my brother's life made him happy and alleviated his terrible grief. I think we all hoped that, with time, things would get better.

Grief can blind you to so much, and make you feel as though nothing worse could possibly happen to you. But good and bad continues, just as life itself does. I often wondered, did we feel buffered by our grief for Mags?

But there were warning signs we missed, and which were glaringly apparent to us years later. My inner voice was one. Deep down, I felt something was amiss with Molly, but I just couldn't put my finger on it. Another warning sign was how Molly hated Jason's friend, Paul, who was incredibly loyal to my brother and never hesitated to tell him what he needed to hear and not what he wanted to hear. Paul was with Jason when they arrived home after a golf trip to see the aftermath of one of Molly's episodes of mental ill-health.

From that moment on, Molly did everything she could to prise Paul out of Jason's life. There was something about Molly that made Paul wary, and he wanted his friend to be careful for the sake of himself and his children. On the day of Jason's wedding to Molly in June 2011, he begged my brother to postpone the proceedings after yet more examples of Molly's lies and fantasies had come to light during the pre-wedding party in Tennessee.

I firmly believe that Molly feigned homesickness to persuade Jason to leave Ireland and move to the US. My brother adored American culture and society. Deep down, I knew he always wondered about forging a life for himself and the children in the US. Perhaps Molly realised this, and homesickness was her way of persuading my brother to opt for a new American life.

By the time of the lavish Tennessee wedding, it was already too late.

Jason and Molly had wed in the US in a civil ceremony several days before the wedding celebration itself. My brother was now working in North Carolina, and had relocated his entire family to the US. He had sold his home in Limerick and put almost all of his savings into the house at Panther Creek Court, just outside Winston-Salem in North Carolina, that Molly had picked out.

During the wedding, Jason was appalled to learn some of the details of Molly's lies. To his horror, she had even claimed to be a pen pal of Mags, and had promised to look after her children if anything happened to her.

Molly had also thrown an embarrassing public tantrum during the wedding celebration itself, and had humiliated Dave in front of all the wedding guests. Jason demanded that she personally apologise the following day, a meeting that unfortunately made matters worse rather than better. When we returned to Ireland, it was almost with a sense of relief. What none of us realised was that Molly's plan had worked to perfection. She had the instant family she wanted, she had separated my brother from his family and his support network in Ireland, and she had persuaded him to move to the US.

Weeks after the wedding, Molly went to a US divorce lawyer to determine her new rights to Jack and Sarah. To her consternation, she was told she had no legal rights. She was not the biological mother of the children, and the only way she would achieve equal rights with Jason was if he signed adoption papers. She had equal rights to all the family property – but the children were Jason's legal responsibility.

That became Molly's next goal.

REMINDER

Getting to know your true self is a critical part of life – but equally as important is recognising that some people can have a negative and toxic impact on our lives.

3

WE ARE NEVER ALONE AND HELPLESS

Molly arrived in our lives at a time when Jason wasn't the only one struggling to make sense of what had happened to Mags. I was caught in a cycle of negativity that began that awful 21 November evening, and which slowly and cunningly dragged me into one of the darkest periods of my life.

Mags's death truly shocked me. I didn't realise it at the time, but the tragedy seemed to trip a switch deep within me. It was as if I had lost a sister. Perhaps it triggered the long-dormant emotions surrounding my lost twin. Whatever the cause, it had an impact on me that was as unexpected as it was challenging.

What struck me to the core of my psyche was the random, unfair nature of what had happened. To see an apparently healthy, devoted wife and mother – in the prime of her life

– taken so suddenly from her husband and children left me grasping for answers. The fact that the tragedy struck without warning made it all the more difficult to accept. I knew she had gone to the doctor days earlier because she felt unwell, but there was no apparent issue with her asthma.

We were told that there was nothing that could have been done, such was the nature of Mags's asthma, the sudden onset of such a severe attack and the cardiac-respiratory pressure she faced that terrible night. The pathologist said Mags's heart was like a ticking time bomb because of her asthma – it could have succumbed to a serious asthma attack at any time, at 19 or 93. But it didn't stop me from wondering whether there was something we had missed. It didn't stop me from questioning how someone so young could die of asthma, and whether there was something, some small indicator we had overlooked.

The shock was greater for me because I suffered from asthma as well, albeit in a milder form. There were periods when I needed a nebuliser once or twice a month. I also had to be hospitalised with my asthma. But Mags had never previously had an attack severe enough to threaten her life. It didn't help that I smoked, a habit I had picked up in my teenage years.

I had never experienced a loss so overwhelming in life before, and I was shocked that I didn't have the answers I needed when I sought them out. I had been brought up with a strong traditional faith but struggled to turn to it when I needed it most. The most dangerous part of such dark sadness is that it turns you against the very things that will help you – almost as if there is nothing better than wallowing in grief and self-pity.

Once the heartbreak and high emotion of Mags's removal, her Requiem Mass and then burial were over, I started to grieve. Or at least I thought I did. In reality, I allowed myself to be sucked into a vortex of damaging emotions and behaviour that initially masqueraded as grief but which ultimately were unmasked as depression.

Over-eating, isolation, brooding and chronic lack of exercise left me floundering in a swamp of negativity. It was only a matter of time before depression set in and, when it did, I was in serious trouble.

I know now that what happened to me was relatively commonplace. It is human nature to take the easier, softer road, rather than the harder, stonier and more challenging path – even though we know in our hearts that the second option is the better one for us in the long run.

The danger of such negative behaviours was apparent from the fact that I had so many things to occupy me – I had my own two children, a busy family life and, of course, the demands of helping Jason with little Jack and Sarah, not to mention my elderly parents. I was never busier in my life. But I still fell prey to such toxic emotions and behaviours.

I am an organised, social person by nature, at my very

best when operating with schedules, work goals and daily dealings with other people. Over the years I learned that I am happiest when involved in projects I believe in. I thrive when, in my personal and business life, I network with others. I like to work to a strict plan.

If you had spoken to me about how I was feeling from 2006 to 2008, I would have said I was simply too busy to be vulnerable to such problems as depression and anxiety. Now, I realise that I confused being busy with having balance in my life. I was deflecting when I needed to take it easier and focus on recovery, healing and positive activity. I dismissed it and buried myself in work and personal tasks.

It was a vicious cycle. The busier I got, the less happy I felt. The more work I took on to try to forget my grief, the worse it was when I suddenly found myself alone with myself. I looked around and saw others devastated at the loss of Mags and committed the cardinal sin of burying my grief – I tried to cope on my own.

Mags had been a part of my everyday life – a constant, daily presence in my world. If I wasn't calling in to see her, she would be calling over to our Raheen home with Jason. If we weren't meeting up, we would be chatting on the phone or texting. There were always social plans being discussed – a meal out, babysitting or even plans for weekends away.

It was only after she was gone that I realised just how much sunshine Mags brought to all our lives. Unconsciously, I came to depend on her for the injection of humour, brightness, positivity and kindness she brought to all of us every day. Mags had become a sounding board for me in life, very much like Jason.

There was now a gaping void left in my daily life, and I simply had no idea what to do about it. It didn't help that, when Mags's loss was brought up in conversation with friends and neighbours, people either tried to quickly move the conversation in a different direction or offered pithy advice such as 'time heals all wounds' or 'give time, time'.

I can understand how people outside our family circle didn't want to appear to intrude on our grief. Looking back, I suspect a lot of people were afraid they would make matters worse for us by talking about Mags's death. Or, perhaps, they were just uncomfortable with talking about such a shocking tragedy in its immediate aftermath and fully aware that a family was still hurting. Some people tried to help, but remarks like 'life moves on' or 'keep yourself busy' offered no comfort and, at times, made me feel awful and inadequate.

Cute little sayings like these might sound nice, but they aren't always true. And in some cases, they are simply devastating for someone who is in pain and feels nothing but a sense of failure when such platitudes don't seem to work or apply to them and their situation. There may be gems of wisdom in them, but only as part of a general recovery process. Far from putting my feet on the grief journey, I was stumbling around without a clear sense of direction or any idea of what to do. Taken together, it all took a toll on me, both mentally and physically.

But it was the physical problems that manifested themselves first. I started comfort eating, usually at night. The more I ate, the worse I felt. Instead of focusing on healthy foods like salads, vegetables, etc., I took to fast food and rich meals like a duck to water. Cakes, biscuits and chocolates became a constant presence in our evenings, as I sat down to watch TV. If I'm honest, food is my Achilles heel – if I'm happy, I like to eat. If I'm sad, I eat to cheer myself up.

When I think back to when it all began with my weight, it was after giving birth. The first time I put on weight was after the birth of my son Dean. I kept the pregnancy weight and added more over the first year or so of his life. I was quite young, and all my friends were out having a good time, socialising and going to college. But I was at home raising a baby at 19 years old with very little money. So I would eat treats as a way to reward myself.

Eventually, I lost all that baby fat with the help of a weight-loss meeting group. It was lovely to meet everyone and have support. Some found the group to be fantastic, but I felt that the pressure to stand on a scale every week was too much of a focus on my weight and not enough on overall well-being. If I had put on a pound or stayed the same weight I felt disappointed with myself.

They say there are horses for courses. The groups have their place, but not in the long term for me. But the eating-reward cycle had been ingrained in my memory, and would prove an issue over the years to come.

Today I understand how a 'sugar rush' works – you get an instant hit from the sugar entering your system, your metabolism gets used to it, then craves another hit and you take a second slice of cake or a few more biscuits. For a brief period, you feel good. But repeat the cycle often enough and you are looking at significant weight gain over a very short period.

The problem was that I indulged in such foods to make myself feel better and achieve a fleeting escape from the pain of loss. It was almost a subconscious thing. Food became an emotional crutch for me.

There is nothing more natural in an Irish home than to sit down together as a family in the evening, brew a pot of tea and munch on a few biscuits, a slice of apple tart or a piece of cake. My problem was the frequency and quantities involved combined with a lack of proper exercise.

It was compounded by the fact that the worse I felt, the more disorganised I became in my daily life and, under time pressure, resorted to takeaways for the family rather than home-cooked meals. It didn't happen every night – but maybe three nights during some weeks. I'd be struggling to juggle work with family commitments and home duties. Under pressure for time, a takeaway was the easiest option, or so I thought. What should have been a treat soon became a weekly expectation.

In the end, I felt worse than when I had started. I developed digestive issues, and was upset at my weight gain. My normal clothes were suddenly all too tight-fitting, and that brought its own feelings of shame and embarrassment. I had always loved fashion, and took pride in my appearance.

Unfortunately, I am not the tallest of people, so I didn't have the height to hide the weight gain, and a few good friends put their concern over hurting my feelings aside and delicately mentioned to me how much weight I had put on and asked me if everything was alright.

So I went on a crash diet – and lost all the weight I had gained. Unfortunately, once I had lost the weight, the cycle inevitably began again – I felt depressed at missing my 'sugar rush', so I 'rewarded' myself for the success of my diet with some treat 'cheats'. Needless to say, all the weight started piling on again. By the time the next diet started, I had put on even more weight than before.

How do you sit down and write about how grief affects your weight? I am not a weight-loss advocate, nor do I want to be. I am sitting here as I write this eating high-protein granola, natural yoghurt, chopped grapes and a drizzle of honey. It is delicious. But I did not eat any of these alone or together until 2019.

I bounced between diets – each more demanding than the

next. But as the weight gain–loss cycle persisted, I lost faith in each one and then moved on to the next. It added instability to the one thing I needed to be stable in my life – my health and well-being.

Physically, I was struggling. I noticed I was having joint pain, so I cut back on what little exercise I was engaged in. It ranked as one of the worst mistakes I made in a cycle of poor decisions. That made the cycle of weight gain and weight loss even more volatile. So I ended up spending more and more time indoors. Instead of being outdoors, where my spirit could draw strength and renewal from nature and the beautiful Limerick and Clare countryside, I was sitting in front of a TV set, feeling depressed and even more likely to overeat once again.

I didn't understand at the time how exercise offers its own natural 'high' to the body through the release of endorphins or 'reward' chemicals following physical exertion. By running, walking and cycling, not only are you getting fitter, healthier and burning off unwanted calories, but your body uses a natural system to make you feel better as a reward. It all adds to your mental well-being.

My weight created a constant battle in my mind. I would antagonise my whole system by eating bad food. I did it regularly, and I did it with each loss I suffered. While I don't want to focus too much on the specifics of my weight gains or losses, there were significant fluctuations of around four stone. Suffice to say, my weight reached a point where it impacted my health, my self-confidence and my general state of mind.

Slowly but surely, the stress was building within me. I didn't realise it, but I was cranking up the pressure on my body with poor decision after poor decision. All my life I had prided myself on my ability to work hard and to 'burn the candle at both ends' in terms of my ability to multitask and achieve high-pressure goals. The problem was that my body's ability to bounce back was steadily being eroded. I felt I just wasn't the same Tracey.

Adding yet another poor decision to the cocktail, I decided I simply couldn't continue at work while feeling so unhappy inside. Almost like the patient who decides to amputate his leg because he has an itchy toe, I resigned from my job despite several colleagues almost begging me to think my decision over. My boss – who became and remains a staunch family friend – even wanted me to take time off to think things through before I made any final commitments.

In some dark recess of my mind, I suspect I thought the break from work would help me. All my decision managed to achieve was to add another layer of anxiety to my already frazzled mind. Now, minus my work income, we suddenly had family financial considerations to take into account. When these dawned on me, I reached rock bottom. I was surrounded by an overwhelming feeling of hopelessness.

It also meant I had even more time on my hands to brood

and fret. While I may not have been myself at work, at least I was working and having a large portion of my day productively occupied. Having eight extra hours a day to wallow in misery was the one thing I hadn't predicted. I felt as if I had let everyone down – Dave, the children, my family, Mags and, most importantly, myself. Not once in my life had I ever considered myself a failure. I had suffered setbacks and disappointments, but had always got up, dusted myself off and worked even harder at achieving my goals. In life, I was a marathon runner and not a sprinter. My life, up until that point, had been lived according to the belief that you only fail when you stop trying.

Now, I truly believed, in the innermost recesses of my soul, that I was a failure for the very first time. It left me feeling devastated. I had tried to run away from grief and pain. In reality, all I was doing was fleeing from life. It had got so bad that I even started avoiding family events – things that I cherished with all my being and usually looked forward to for weeks in advance.

Guilt made it almost unbearable. I looked at Jason and saw suffering etched on every fibre of his being. I knew his every waking moment was a struggle without Mags. Everything in his life he cared for appeared to remind him of what he had lost. I knew that to cope, he felt he needed to be close to her spirit and memory – hence the time he would spend at her grave.

Jason was bravely trying to rebuild his shattered life for his two young children. Looking at him, I felt guilty for feeling so bad when his suffering seemed to me to be on an altogether different plane. It was probably one of the only times in my life that I didn't confide in him. How could I possibly have? My brother had a sufficiently heavy burden to bear after Mags's death that I couldn't worry him with my own problems, or so I felt. Pain and loss are deeply personal, and I committed the ridiculous act of comparing rather than identifying. I found myself trapped in a dark place that I never dreamed I would inhabit. My health was in shambles. I was hurt and suffering.

Each day left me feeling scared and isolated, as well as completely and utterly hopeless. Worst of all, my pride kept me from reaching out, speaking honestly about how I felt and accepting any help offered. I had two sons, aged five and fifteen, who needed me, but I wasn't my best self by any stretch of the imagination. I was lost.

When people with my best interests at heart tried to help me, to coax me out of the darkness I was trapped in and lead me safely back into the light, I lashed out. I used anger as a defence mechanism and, to my shame, I hurt some of the people I loved most on this earth. Even now, years later, it pains me to recall those moments. I was far from proud of myself. My anger then quickly faded to reveal a deep sense of guilt for hurting those I loved so dearly. In truth, I acted out of fear and embarrassment at the place I found myself stuck in.

In turn, I tended to increasingly isolate myself – to push my loved ones away, to keep them at arm's length lest I hurt them further. All I was doing was feeding and deepening my depression. Hopeless, helpless and afraid, I felt I had nowhere to turn.

In the end, a smile was my only defence mechanism on occasions. If you smile then people will think, 'Oh, thank God, she's fine, she's grand, and we can all go back to normal.' My smile was my mask, but as the pain got greater, even that smile began to crack.

My husband had been desperately trying to pierce the fog of negativity and depression surrounding me. We've been together since we were teenagers, and Dave knows me better than anyone. He knew something was wrong despite my insistence that everything would be OK and that I was simply working through some grief issues. Dave knew I was in trouble.

He had gently tried to help at the beginning with suggestions about positive things for me to do, or by encouraging me to re-engage with old friends. He felt if I started doing the things that made the old Tracey happy, it would help lift me. But, as I sank further into apathy, he dropped gentleness for firm action.

Later, he admitted to me he was very worried. Dave was extremely close to Jason – they were almost like brothers – and he had done everything he could to support him after

Mags's death. I was shocked when, much later, Dave revealed he was almost more worried for me than he was for Jason during that period.

Dave strongly suggested I go for professional help in the form of counselling. It was more of a direction than a request. Initially, I was totally against it. 'There is nothing wrong with me,' I told myself. 'I'm simply in mourning. A bit of a down patch, but that's all.' I also tried to persuade myself that it would pass in time. Yet somewhere deep inside I knew I needed help. The pain was getting so bad that I realised I needed to take action.

I visited my GP and they organised a referral to a counsellor. Reluctantly, I went along to the appointment, but I had all my defence mechanisms in place. My story was simple – I was still mourning my sister-in-law and I was a bit down but my friends and family were overreacting. I didn't really need counselling, just a bit of time to myself.

The counsellor was a very nice woman who did a taping and visualisation session. But it just wasn't right for me. The signs weren't good from the beginning – I struggled to find her house in the days long before Google Maps and, when I finally arrived after getting lost several times, I was stressed and didn't benefit from the session.

My defence mechanisms made the process much harder than it ought to have been. I didn't feel a connection between us. But Dave and my family weren't allowing any withdrawal from the process, so I agreed to try a different counsellor. It was largely the same result. I wouldn't lower my barriers, the counsellor was polite, helpful and kind, but I didn't feel any benefit from the process.

The second counsellor was a really lovely gentleman. He had a kindly manner and gently tried to get me to open up about what was going on in my life. Later, defensive as always, I told my husband when he asked how the session had gone that the counsellor was very nosy and I found that quite off-putting.

Dave suggested I give it another try, and I went back for a second session. This time I told the counsellor that I had a work event that evening and that he was not to make me cry, as I didn't want to arrive at the function with red-rimmed eyes. Kindly, the counsellor suggested that maybe I wasn't ready for the work we needed to do together? He was right – in fact, they were all right.

Reluctantly, I agreed to try a third counsellor. Suddenly, things began to change. I'm convinced they understood from the minute I walked through the office door what was going on. I still tried my usual defensive act – offering the minimum of information, telling the counsellor what I felt they wanted to hear and trying to keep the spotlight firmly off the issues I was anxious and embarrassed about. But they saw right through my defence walls and persisted with the process of getting me to open up.

Even though everything was far from alright in my life, I tried to put a brave face on things and maintain a happy outer demeanour. In counselling terms, I had already wedged my game mask firmly in place. The first step in my recovery would be removing the mask and being honest about how I felt. The very first person I needed to be honest with was myself.

My counsellor wasn't buying any of my bullshit. They gently engaged with me and, almost despite myself, I felt slowly drawn into the conversation. It helped that I felt a connection with the counsellor, as if this was someone I could like and trust. If we were in a different context, the counsellor was a person I reckoned I could become friends with.

Bit by bit, almost like peeling back the layers of an onion, I began to open up. It was slow and painful, but gradually my defence barriers began to descend. The counsellor was shrewd enough not to force the pace of our chats. I was allowed to dictate the pace of the conversations and how much information I shared about myself. It was painful at first, I was hesitant about revealing the full extent of my emotions, fears and anxieties.

The more I opened up, the faster the pace of progress became. As the sessions passed, I felt increasingly comfortable with the process and, almost unbelievably, I began to look forward to the next session. For the first time in months, my family noticed there were times I had a genuine smile on my face.

Eventually, it reached a point where, like a log dam breaking, it all came pouring out. To use a medical analogy, the boil of my grief and depression had finally been lanced, and all the pus of negative feelings, like fear, anxiety and self-doubt, came seeping out.

Yes, it was that ugly.

There were counselling sessions where I wept, where I raged at the world and where I confided my fears about the future. There were times I shook with emotion. But, it slowly dawned on me that I was now leaving the sessions feeling lighter than when I first came in. I reckon that counsellor needed a lot of their own counselling after seeing me!

Gradually, bit by bit, I started to feel stronger. I had to move forward in my life, and I was determined to do all the suggested things in terms of assisting that process. I started listening to podcasts of inspirational talks, I engaged with mindfulness, I tried meditation and I took yoga classes.

I got lost for so long that I forgot how to find myself. But being shown the path to recovery and healing was like the storm clouds parting and being offered a glimpse of sunshine in the uplands beyond.

A key part of my recovery – and I hope it will be for yours too – was realising that we can be products of our surroundings. If we surround ourselves with negativity, fear and anxiety, is it any surprise that our thoughts slowly become more negative? I have a very good friend who is in Alcoholics

Anonymous, and they once told me a key concept with their fellowship is to 'stick with the winners'.

I had tried to cut myself off from the winners in my life – my family, friends and workmates – to wallow lonely and isolated in my own personal pit of grief. It had all but broken me. Now, I started to work out a new life plan determined to harness the positives in my life.

In tandem with that, I also had to start to distance myself from people who weren't good for me. There were some around me who, while likely meaning well, had offered advice that proved very negative for me. Others encouraged behaviour that wasn't good for me. In hindsight, I don't know whether these people genuinely believed what they were advising me, or whether they simply didn't have my best interests at heart.

I also came to understand that a dangerous part of my personality was a tendency to be a people-pleaser. Like thousands before me, I began to understand that the most difficult word to learn to say is 'no'. Just to keep other people happy, I would agree to certain arrangements or plans that I myself wasn't happy with. Ultimately, I paid the price for it.

Learning to say 'no' was hard. There are times to this day that I find it difficult – but I am acutely aware of it now. Some decisions were painful, and I know some people were offended by my stance. But I had to do what was right for me. It was difficult, and it was painful, but it was the correct thing to do.

It wasn't all doom and gloom. People who loved me and genuinely did have my best interests at heart, such as Dave, my siblings and my parents, thought I wanted to do some of these things of my own will – and only later came to understand that I was doing them to please others, and not myself.

In my life, I had made great friends, and these were the ones who stood by me and supported me. Others had experienced similar problems and, once they realised I was struggling, privately shared their experiences with me – something that offered tremendous solidarity.

You will note me referring to solidarity many times. The truth is that I believe it cannot be underestimated. There is enormous solidarity in realising you are not alone or unique when facing up to problems. On the other hand, some people were happy to have me working hard to help them at the cost of my own well-being; when I began to ease back, they resented it. As a result, a few close relationships over time became a bit more distant.

It is a difficult concept to comprehend, that not all adults are grown-ups – and some people are fake; that the person on the outside is a sham, a façade, and the inner person is not as warm, kind-hearted and generous as you've been led to believe. Ultimately, they are selfish and want you only for what you can do for them. Slowly, I began to learn that it is better to gauge people by their actions rather than their words.

In the same way, I am the product of my own actions. Children look to us, and our actions are what they judge us by. Our actions speak louder than any words possibly can in giving children an example. So why should adults be any different?

The most powerful realisations are often the simplest. I learned that one definition of insanity is to keep doing the same thing over and over again while all the time expecting a different outcome. I wasn't happy with aspects of my life, and it wasn't until I started changing things as part of my life reboot that I got back to being the Tracey I wanted to be.

Along with the ongoing counselling sessions, I was advised to make some simple changes in my life, including my diet, lifestyle and social life. All were aimed at removing negative influences from my life and, instead, surrounding me with a safety net of positivity, solidarity and support.

Some were easier to do than others. The first change was my diet. I cut out all the junk food and started to have a healthy breakfast, lunch and dinner. The emphasis was on foods that would boost my system – lots of vegetables, salads and fish, while also including meat for protein. There was to be no 'grazing' between meals. If I needed a treat at night, it was in the shape of fresh fruit.

There were times it was hard. Some nights I went to bed practically dreaming about a slice of cake or a few biscuits, but I stuck to my regime. One thing I learned is that you have to harness your own individual strengths. One of my strengths was planning. When I knew I had a plan, I became determined to stick with it.

I started cooking a lot more. The emphasis was on fresh ingredients, healthy foods and home-cooked meals. Not only was I going to benefit, but the entire family would feel better as a result. We all loved takeaways, but we made the decision that these would be confined to the weekend – and would be considered a special treat. So if we had an Indian, Thai or Chinese takeaway on a Saturday night, it was a home-cooked meal for Sunday. It was too easy to fall into a routine of saying that, because Dave and I were both working, a takeaway was acceptable for three, four or even five nights a week.

In some ways, I was becoming a version of my mother. When I was young, my mam placed enormous emphasis on providing good food for us – and God help you if you didn't eat your dinner. She often left me to sit at the table for hours to finish my plate of stew (which I hated), no matter my pleas that I'd eaten enough dinner. It was always important in our house to 'clear your plate'. It may have taken 30 years and then some to realise that I just need to eat enough for me to be healthy.

Ever the student, I started researching foods and the particular benefits each offered: fatty fish can help fight depression; dark chocolate in small amounts helps with blood flow to the brain and thereby delivers positive moods;

fermented foods help with gut health, which is one of the key issues with stress; bananas literally can 'turn a frown upside down'; and oats help promote a more even release of sugars from the bloodstream, thereby helping promote balance and a feeling of well-being.

By April 2018, I was taking my nutrition very seriously. It may seem obvious, but I had to come to realise that an engine is only as good as the fuel you put into it. There is also so much inspiration from the large number of women and men just like me looking to help each other and share healthy recipes.

I always liked seafood, and it became a cornerstone of my new healthy regimen. Salmon, crab claws, prawns and other types of fish and shellfish became a staple of my diet. Each meal featured lots of healthy vegetables or salads. Chicken, sweet corn and noodle soup is a staple of our winter diet. We also experimented with healthy foreign foods, such as halloumi, which the children came to adore.

The second change was exercise. Most importantly, I resumed walking. Some friends had suggested I go to a gym for the social aspect of exercising in a group, but I loved nature, and simply smelling the cut grass or the hedges after a heavy rainfall while out walking was almost a tonic in itself. There is nothing like noticing the changing seasons in nature to remind you of the cycles of life.

I made it a point to exercise daily. Sometimes it was literally a stroll around our estate in Raheen. Other times I'd meet a friend and we'd go for a longer walk, either along the bank of the River Shannon or around Limerick city centre.

As my body trimmed down and I got healthier, my mind began to slowly clear itself of the fog that had enveloped it. I got sharper and more focused in my thinking – I suddenly realised I could see the path I needed to get back on. My life had always been about work, whether in the home or the workplace, and I knew I needed to get back out there.

A third change was to find time for positive things, especially activities with my family and friends. I was blessed with both and, when I needed them, both were there for me. I agreed to go on social nights with my girlfriends, I went to the cinema with Dave and the children, we went out for meals to mark special occasions and, best of all, we started organising weekend breaks in my beloved Clare near Spanish Point.

I can't overstate how important these outings were. They reminded me of who I really was. It was as if I had a seat in a time machine and travelled back to an era where my happiest memories were forged. Clare was where I had spent the most joyous days of my childhood. Simply being there was like having an intravenous injection of happiness and optimism into my system. It was a lesson I have tried never to forget.

Nothing banishes the darkness like the light – and the light of memory is one of the warmest that we can utilise.

Family was the anchor of my life, and I rediscovered the awesome power it offers us if we only harness it. The unquestioning love and support of my parents, brothers and sister felt like a warm, protective blanket being wrapped around me. If I'm honest, I felt a little foolish that I hadn't realised this support had been there for me all along. Sometimes in our grief we just miss what is right there in front of our faces.

Jack and Sarah had always been a part of our lives, but I now started including them in almost everything we did. No longer did I have any black cloud of duty overshadowing my involvement with Jason, Jack and Sarah. It was like discovering an unopened gift after Christmas – I had these three incredible people to share my life with. They were a gorgeous family and we adored having the three of them in our home. It helped enormously that our children, Dean and Adam, doted on Jack and Sarah, and were constantly campaigning for them to be allowed over. Adam was just a few years older than Jack and, in a short time, was almost like an older brother to Jason's son.

I slowly realised that, by helping others, we take the focus off ourselves and leave less room for self-pity. It may seem hard to understand, but helping Jason with Jack and Sarah actually benefited me more than it did him or the children.

Throughout it all, I was blessed with the support of my immediate and extended family. I wasn't the only one who deeply felt the loss of Mags. My sister Marilyn had been quite friendly with Mags and her sister Catherine. She was also devastated by the tragedy. So many had lost so much, and we found comfort and drew strength from one another.

Marilyn mourned in her own way. She realised that I was struggling badly, and did her level best to help me. When she learned that I was attending a counsellor, Marilyn couldn't have been more supportive, and suggested that, when I felt strong enough, we should consider a wellness break together. In hindsight, I think Marilyn wanted to offer me a positive goal as something to work towards.

By April 2007, I had made great strides and was feeling happy and confident in myself, so Marilyn and I organised a health break in Portugal. What neither of us realised was just how serious the resort involved took the commitment to health and well-being.

We arrived in the Algarve – just up the road from Praia da Luz – on 1 May to beautiful, balmy early summer weather. Then we discovered that not only would we be subjected to a strict dietary regime while staying at the resort, but there was a special programme of exercise. I love walking and the outdoors but, to our horror, we realised that this was more like a training camp for Olympic athletes.

The menus were all vegan. Despite my commitment to a healthy diet, I found myself fantasising about fillet steaks and fish and chips. We were awoken at six in the morning to drink lemon and hot water as some kind of purifying procedure before being directed to yoga by sunrise.

Marilyn was supportive, but by the third day she was quietly cursing me as we were dispatched on a mid-morning 10km hike with nothing for lunch but a vegetable broth. My sister's idea of a wellness break was that we were now fully entitled to a relaxation day with poolside massage and cocktails.

A couple of days into our stay Jason rang, and it was the first time I had heard him laugh in months. He thought the prospect of Marilyn and myself being force-fed salads and pulses before being marched out on hikes was absolutely hilarious. So much for my idea of a wellness break packed with spa treatments, sunbathing and massages.

But there was nothing funny about the timing of our break. I discovered on the second day that one of the guests on the break was a UK-based journalist. Three days into the wellness programme, she informed the organisers that she may have to leave early. She had just been contacted by her editors about a young British girl who had gone missing in the Algarve.

Later, as Marilyn and myself walked through Praia da Luz, we were taken by the fact that every street sign and telegraph pole seemed to be covered with posters of a missing child. I also thought there were a lot of Portuguese police around the resort. Later, we discovered that the missing child was Madeleine McCann.

In the almost 15 years since then, I've never been able to get the image of Madeleine and her parents, Kate and Gerry,

Mam and Dad were married for 61 years. They wed in St. Joseph's Church, Limerick, on St. Stephen's Day in 1959, which is why Dave and I chose St. Stephen's Day to renew our vows.

Left to right: me, Mam, Jason and Wayne. We spent every summer in Spanish Point.

Christmas day was always spent in my house, but sometimes we would head away for a few days together. In this picture, taken in December 2003, Marilyn, Jason and I are in Mayo.

David's mother, Norah, and our first-born, Dean, in 1992. Norah was one of the wittiest people I knew. She would pop down and look after our kids when Dave and I wanted to have some time together.

Mags and Jason on Jack's birthday.

I took this picture in September 2017 as the sun set on Jack, Adam and Sarah. They were oblivious that night was setting in and were so engrossed in having fun together. Dave and I watched them for hours. These are the moments we treasure.

This picture was taken by our good friend Dermot Culhane at our vow renewal. It was one of the most special and memorable days of my life.

At the Midwest Cancer Foundation charity ball in October 2019. Earlier that day, I felt anxious and wasn't sure about socialising. It turned out to be a fantastic evening supporting a good cause with one of my oldest childhood friends.

Dave's 50th birthday dinner at Adare Manor. This was a time where life was going well for us all. I felt really confident in myself, hence the selfie in the pink suit!

My mother's death in May 2020 left a void in our lives. She was the fulcrum of our family and my biggest supporter. I try to live my live being all the good things she was.

This photo was taken during the last holiday Mam had. Mam and Dad loved to revisit Spanish point so we would all go and stay there a few times a year. It became a place where we all would come together after Jason died. Left to right: Jack, Mam Adam and Sarah.

This image was taken at our son Dean's wedding to Kelly Fitzgerald in August 2021. We didn't realise it was being taken. I think it captures the shared moment of peace and happiness we were feeling surrounded by family.

Left to right: Dr Lisa O'Rourke-Scott, me and Colin Healy on board the *Ilen* (Ireland's oldest sailing ship) in June 2021. 'Sailing into Wellness' is a fantastic programme that empowers individuals to build skills on the water that are transferable to everyday life.

During the pandemic, I, like so many, home-schooled the children. One project I set for Sarah was about the benefits of sea swimming and the Wim Hof method. We swam daily from September 2020 to May 2021 – it was as cold as we look but a must-try!

out of my mind. I've lost count of the times I prayed that they would find their daughter. It also taught me a very valuable life lesson. No matter how badly off you think you are, the chances are that there is someone else with problems far, far worse than the ones you are struggling with.

Slowly, I rediscovered the joy in my life. Where once I had been plagued by fear, anxiety and negativity, I now had hope, joy, laughter and was looking to the future. It was as if a pair of blinkers had been shed from my eyes, and I was looking at the world in clear, properly focused vision.

Despite this, I decided to stick with the counselling sessions, because I found them so helpful. In a matter of months, I didn't just feel like the old Tracey – I felt like the new, improved and upgraded version of Tracey. My life would now be lived according to a support plan. In future years, I would need that support plan more than I ever could have dreamed.

There were shocking, unexpected setbacks. In August 2007, we lost Dave's mother, Norah, in the most upsetting of circumstances. She had been a rock of support for us since Mags's death, particularly over that Christmas, when, almost single-handedly, she had worked miracles in trying to provide some kind of festive lift for us.

November and December 2006 had been brutal months. There was a bleakness that I just couldn't seem to escape – and

I still struggle to think about how we managed to get through that awful Christmas. We were desperate to try to offer some kind of festive season for the children – both ours and Jason's. But that was very hard when Mags, who had seemed the very embodiment of the Christmas spirit, was gone, leaving a searing, aching void where she should have been.

But Norah was irrepressible. She was single-minded about making Christmas for the children and, somehow, her infectious humour and inherent kindness rubbed off on us adults. It was one of the bleakest Christmas seasons of my life. But it would have been far, far worse but for Dave's mother.

Norah was a young woman, being just 67 years old. When Dave and I were young parents with our eldest, Dean, Norah had been an incredible support to us and had been a fixture in our lives as our family expanded with the later arrival of Adam. No matter the family celebration or occasion, Norah would be there to add her special type of sparkle to the event.

On 8 August 2007, Dave and I decided to call over to her house before going to see Jason and the children. Dave had been trying to contact his mother since the previous day, but he hadn't been able to get through. He just wanted to check on her, say 'hello' and catch up on any family news.

Arriving at her house, we walked up to the front door and rang the doorbell, without reply. We kept ringing the doorbell and knocking on the door, but to no avail. Dave decided to call over to see one of the neighbours to ask if they knew anything about Norah's movements. Norah was a very active woman, who went swimming and walking and was a regular attendee at Mass. She was also meticulous about maintaining her husband's grave.

The neighbours couldn't shed any light on where Norah was. They hadn't heard anything about her heading away for a day trip or even a short break. We hadn't talked to her in a few days, so we couldn't completely rule out the possibility that maybe she had gone away for the day and simply forgotten to tell us. I tried ringing her phone one more time but, as it rang, it suddenly cut out – as if the handset battery had died.

Deep within me, my inner voice was murmuring that something wasn't right. But it was only a gut instinct – I had nothing specific to go on. That proved prophetic when, sometime later, with family members still unable to contact Norah, a neighbour went to the property amid growing concern for her welfare. Again, there was no answer to repeated knocks on the front door.

Deciding to peer through the letterbox for any sign of activity, they were horrified to spot Norah lying on the floor inside. Paramedics and Gardaí were called, but nothing could be done for her. Norah was believed to have suffered a heart attack in bed, and another while descending the stairs from her bedroom, perhaps to call for help or to get a drink for herself.

The scale of the tragedy was exacerbated by the fact that Norah had been eagerly anticipating the marriage of her youngest son, Paul, in Italy in September. Norah idolised Paul, and it was a family occasion everyone was looking forward to. For Dave and myself, that wedding offered a chance to escape the gloom of life after Mags, even if only for a few days.

Instead of a wedding, we now had another funeral to prepare for, as Dave's family would come together from England, Canada and the United States to mourn Norah and give her a fitting send-off. After the loss of Mags just 10 months before, it was another shattering blow for our family.

Over time, I came to understand the terrible misconception that you eventually get over a loss – that, over time, you put it in the past and slowly forget about it. The truth is you don't. No matter how hard you try, the grief will always be there. What I learned was that the process of recovery revolved around learning to live with our loss and our grief. Over time, the memories of our lost loved ones stop being painful recollections and somehow transform into mind treasures. You slowly become grateful for having had them in your life rather than only being heartbroken at their loss. Allowing this process to occur is what it means to be properly grieving.

In a way, the death of a loved one shocks us, because it reminds us of our own mortality. Many people work on ensuring they are not afraid of dying. In reality, what all of us should be focused on is making sure we are not afraid of living – that we fully embrace the opportunities and challenges that life puts in our way.

I learned that the person I needed to understand most in life was myself. The most important introduction I needed was to the real me – to discover what Tracey wanted, what made Tracey happy and what Tracey was good at.

Over time, I also discovered that not everyone deserves to know the real me. People with negative outlooks or selfish priorities should be allowed to criticise who they think I am – but I need to distinguish between the real me and the person they think I am.

REMINDER

Never forget the link between the mind and body – if you look after your physical well-being with healthy, positive activities, it will help enormously to mind your mind.

4

IT IS RIGHT TO FIGHT FOR THOSE
WE LOVE

Some losses are so severe, so painful that just thinking about them – even years later – can make you physically wince. It is almost as if part of you is missing and the simple mention of that person's name instantly reminds you of the loss – and all the pain comes flooding back to fill the raw void they left in your life.

When you lose a loved one in the most horrifically violent circumstances imaginable, the pain goes to a different level. How do you try to make sense of their loss when they died at the hands of people they should have been able to trust, people they loved – and the fight for justice then drags on for years? Closure takes a firm second place to the demand for truth and justice.

On 2 August 2015, I received a phone call that told me that

my brother Jason had been killed. I was on holiday in France with Dave and the children when the grim news came. Even now I remember the stark contrast – the joy of a holiday, the warm French sun, the anticipation of fun-filled days to come and then, suddenly, it was as if someone flicked a switch and the colour drained, leaving only a world of darkness filled with pain and grief.

Dave took the call that evening. Looking back, I don't know if it was my inner voice giving me advance warning, but I knew immediately as the phone rang that something was terribly wrong. I remember watching Dave's face and seeing him anxiously glance over at me, concern etched on his features. He simply said, 'Tracey, it's Jason … listen to me, Jason is dead.'

After all that had happened with Mags, I couldn't believe it. It just wasn't fair – not again. And not for someone as kind, gentle and loving as Jason. For a few minutes, the emotion was just too much, and I wept tears of pure anguish. I struggled to hold things together, as much for Dave as for the children. Thankfully, the coping part of my character knew there was important work to be done, and it came to the fore.

Instantly, I wanted details about what had happened. Before a word was said to me, I wondered if it was a car crash. Or some kind of accident? Jason was a very careful driver, so I thought a traffic accident was unlikely. I knew that North Carolina had a high gun ownership rate, but

Jason didn't work in a cash business, so he would never have been a target for a robbery, and he didn't frequent the areas where the shootings largely occurred. Deep within me I knew something else was involved – something dark, sinister and alien to the world of our tight-knit family.

We received only scant details from our family back in Limerick, who had themselves only received a terse phone call from Molly's mother, Sharon, in the US. The initial information was that Jason had died from a head injury suffered in a fall after being pushed by Molly during some kind of domestic incident at their Panther Creek Court home.

Repeated attempts by our family to obtain more details from the US failed. I knew something was very badly amiss, so I started calling all the numbers I had for Jason's in-laws in the US. Eventually, I managed to get through to Sharon Martens. She told me Jason had been drinking for almost 24 hours and had got into a fight with Molly. In her version, Jason had attacked Molly and, as she shoved him away, he fell and struck his head, sustaining fatal injuries in the process.

I listened in growing disbelief as she unleashed a stream of invective about how Jason had been abusive to Molly and claimed (falsely, as it later transpired) that the Davidson County Police had been called on six occasions to the family home because of domestic incidents. She didn't offer details of what had happened so much as a condemnation of the person my brother was. Sharon was cold, almost matter-of-fact on the line – not a shred of sorrow detectable in her voice over Jason's death.

The only emotion she displayed came when, in response to Sharon Martens comment that her daughter was at the sheriff's department, I asked if Molly had been arrested. That seemed to provoke her anger, and she challenged me, saying how dare I ask such a thing about her daughter. Sharon then hung up. All efforts to ring back failed, and I knew I had to get to North Carolina as quickly as possible.

Alone we are vulnerable but, supported by a loving and devoted family, we are powerful beyond measure. Dave was almost like a brother to Jason, but he put his own shock and grief aside to support me in doing what I knew I had to do. He booked me a flight back to Ireland and then drove me five hours to Charles de Gaulle airport in Paris. In a supportive embrace, he told me to look after Jason's children, Jack and Sarah, in North Carolina. Dave said he would look after our children and everything at home in Ireland while I raced to the US. He told me what I needed to hear: 'Tracey, go and do what needs to be done.'

Even now, years later, I remember the stress and anxiety of those desperate hours. The repeated attempts to get information from North Carolina about the true circumstances of Jason's death, desperately trying to charge my mobile phone at the airport and also to make flight arrangements for the trip from Ireland to the US.

Molly wasn't answering her phone. Eventually, I sent her a text saying that if she didn't return my calls I would personally start ringing every neighbour in her estate for information. Minutes later, my phone rang and a tearful Molly proceeded to lie through her teeth about Jason drunkenly attacking her and then accidentally dying after she pushed him and he fell backwards, striking the back of his head in the process.

It was an act, and a poor one at that. By now I was familiar with Molly's tendency to bend the truth and go on flights of pure fantasy, all to make herself the centre of attention. I had no time for her antics now. Molly sounded very nervous and was deeply unwilling to be drawn into the specifics of what had happened. I knew there was more to the story than that, but, despite my questions, I got no further details from her.

My priority was now Jack and Sarah, and I demanded to be allowed to speak with Jack. When he came on the line, I could hear the hesitancy in his little voice, as if he was afraid to say too much in front of those around him. 'Hey Jacko, it's Tracey, love. I am so sorry. I love you both and I will be over soon,' I vowed to him. The call was then cut off.

Adrenalin is a wonderful asset but also a dangerous friend. Over the next few days, it was pure adrenalin and the support of my family and friends that saw me endure the unendurable. I had to get to the US, but first, I had to fight a legal battle to stop Jason's body from being cremated before I even arrived in North Carolina, and then I had to fight just to be able to view his remains. My family only won that right when we agreed to foot the entire funeral costs – a condition the Martens family demanded in writing.

Molly and her family staged an impromptu memorial service in North Carolina for Jason, which we were warned we were not allowed to attend. Her family even hired private security guards to ensure we couldn't gain access. When we arrived at Jason's old home hoping for information, the police were immediately called.

I spoke multiple times with the Davidson County Police Department over the following days and weeks, and I got the impression that they were slowly coming to the view that my brother's death involved more than a tragic domestic incident. Viewing my brother's broken and battered body in the funeral home had been traumatic – not even the skill of the morticians had been able to mask the appalling violence he had been subjected to.

Molly and her father, Tom, a retired FBI agent, had insisted Jason attacked them that evening. Tom portrayed himself to the police as a hero who had saved his adored daughter by courageously confronting his drunken Irish son-in-law in an upstairs bedroom at their home. Tom and his wife, Sharon, had arrived unexpectedly for a visit – and Tom had brought a metal baseball bat that he said he had bought as a gift for Jack. The bat had been in the downstairs bedroom where Tom and Sharon were sleeping when he claimed he was awoken by a row upstairs and, grabbing the bat, went up to investigate.

The problem was that their story didn't match the physical evidence at the scene, though I didn't know this at the time. My brother had essentially been pulverised. Later, I learned he had been asleep in bed when he was attacked with the bat and a concrete paving block. Toxicology tests would reveal an attempt had even been made to drug him.

Jason was found, naked and soaked in blood, on the bedroom floor. One of the most upsetting things I later learned was that police believed Molly and Tom had deliberately delayed making a call to emergency services just to ensure Jason was dead when paramedics and police arrived. Paramedics noted his body was cold to the touch – and reported this, indicating that the death had occurred much earlier than indicated. Later, detectives would suspect that an audio recording of Tom and Molly giving CPR to Jason was no more than an act for the benefit of the emergency call operator on the line.

Desperate as I was for the truth to be known about the precise circumstances of my brother's death, I had a more pressing priority – securing the safety of Jason's two children. Within hours of arriving in North Carolina, I realised I faced a legal battle to wrest Jack and Sarah from Molly's custody. Molly had immediately commenced legal proceedings to secure permanent custody of the two children.

Incredible as it may seem, while a murder investigation by Davidson County Police Department into the actions of Molly and Tom was slowly evolving, Jack and Sarah had been placed in Molly's custody. The children were only interviewed by the North Carolina Department of Social Services (DSS) after they had been several days in the custody of Molly and her family. Even more remarkably, the children knew that after their social services interviews they would be returned to Molly's care – hardly an incentive to contradict the story already concocted by Molly and Tom about what had happened to their father.

Jack and Sarah had been left orphaned by the murder of their father. Worse still, they were warned by Molly that if they went back to Ireland they would never again be able to see or talk to their friends. Going to Ireland, where they had lived for the first five to six years of their lives, was portrayed as some kind of punishment.

My concerns about Jack and Sarah's well-being were raised directly with the DSS. They told me they had a 'safety plan' in place for the children but, beyond Molly being told not to leave North Carolina, in my opinion it was little more than bureaucratic box-ticking. DSS also bluntly told me that issues over us not being able to see Jack and Sarah were nothing to do with them – and were entirely up to Molly.

I was blessed to secure the services of a great lawyer, Kim Bonuomo, who would ultimately help us win our fight to secure custody of Jack and Sarah. We were also fortunate to have an insightful and compassionate judge in Brian Shipwash to hear the custody case. The case had by now attracted major headlines not just in our native Ireland but also across the US.

Fortunately, we were able to draw on a good circle of friends for support and advice – not to mention a series of experts who explained to us the importance of the media, diplomatic services and Irish-American networks. The media would play a key role for us – highlighting the true circumstances of what had happened to Jason, confronting the lies being told about him by Molly and her friends and, more importantly, maintaining an unrelenting focus on the case.

The profile the case received ultimately resulted in several major breakthroughs. Molly's history of mental health issues was highlighted to the court for the custody hearing, despite her trying to minimise them. After the hearing, her former boyfriend, Keith Maginn, courageously came forward and outlined the scale of Molly's psychiatric battles. While Molly claimed to the court that her bipolar assessment as a teenager was effectively a misdiagnosis, Keith revealed that she had been on up to 16 types of medication a day when they were living together. Just months before she travelled to Ireland to work as a nanny for Jason's children, she had been admitted to a Georgia mental health facility. Keith admitted he came forward because he was concerned for the welfare of Jack and Sarah.

Despite all the revelations, the DSS were not willing to petition for Jack and Sarah to be removed from Molly's custody. We would have to win the court battle if Jason's wishes were to be honoured and his children were to be given to the protection of his Irish family, as he had so carefully detailed in his will. The specific details of Jason's will – where he made Dave and myself the guardians of his children, rather than Molly – came as a huge blow to Molly during the custody hearing.

Some of Molly's friends tried to portray her as a 'SuperMom', and Molly herself gave emotional evidence to the hearing about 'my children'. She insisted she had raised Sarah from when she was a baby and was the only mother she had ever known. Members of our extended family had travelled to North Carolina, and they were able to offer a very different picture of Molly and her behaviour. Ultimately, enough information had emerged to persuade the court to grant us custody of Jack and Sarah, a decision that came as a seismic shock to Molly, who had assumed she would win custody.

In my life, I don't think I have ever experienced relief such as I felt the day Jason's children were returned to us on foot of that court order. On 17 August 2015, I went to a DSS office with Dave to take Jack and Sarah into our care – I knelt to hug the two of them, and it was the greatest grief antidote anyone could imagine.

I was heartbroken, exhausted and emotionally fragile. But those tearful hugs with Jack and Sarah were a welcome reminder of all that is good in life. A reassurance that light can banish the dark and that hope can quell fear. Everything we had endured over the past terrible fortnight had been worth it, just to embrace those two children and promise them that everything would be alright.

Our trip home was literally a case of planes, trains and automobiles. On 20 August, our plane finally landed at Shannon Airport. After all of the heartbreak of the previous weeks, it was a welcome chance to draw breath. But my relief was tempered by the realisation that I now had Jason's funeral to face in just five days.

A huge support at that time was the Kevin Bell Repatriation Trust (KBRT). Established by the family of Kevin Bell, from Newry, Co. Down, who had died, aged 26, in a hit-and-run tragedy in New York in 2013, the KBRT were instrumental in helping us to get Jason back to Limerick – and not to be overawed by the costs involved. When families are struggling to cope with grief, groups such as KBRT truly rank as angels on earth.

Years later, I remember parts of Jason's funeral only in blurred images – the huge crowds, the upset at seeing the grave opened to allow Jason to be reunited with his beloved Mags, the overwhelming sense of loss and the near terror of what the future held.

Mags's sister, Catherine, told me that two white butterflies had fluttered together over the grave. She felt it was a sign of Jason and Mags being reunited. I recall hoping and praying that it was true. My feelings were a toxic mix of loss, pain and fury at what had been done to my brother. But there was also a steely determination that justice would be done for him.

If I had a crystal ball and could have seen into the future, I'd have despaired at the tortured road we would be asked to travel. For the next 18 months, Dave and I faced a wearying and costly routine of flying to North Carolina for regular updates on the investigation, meetings to help police and prosecutors and an unrelenting legal process over Jason's estate. Molly fought us every step of the way over Jason's estate and, at one point, had even attempted to sell off the contents of the Panther Creek Court home. When we visited with Jack and Sarah for a court hearing in November 2019, one aim was for the children to be allowed to sort through what they wished to ship back to Ireland from their former home. We discovered on arrival that Molly's uncle had emptied the storage unit of all but the basic contents in the days after the settlement of the wrongful death action. There was little or nothing of the children's former life left for them.

Worse still, we also faced the realisation that Molly and her family had no intention of leaving us alone because we had custody of the children. We had a meeting with the Gardaí over the fact that Jack and Sarah were considered potential 'snatch' risks – and a special police response plan was put in place for any such eventuality.

We learned that neighbours and even the families of children attending the same schools as Jack and Sarah in Limerick were suddenly 'friended' on social media from people in the US we soon discovered were close to Molly. They were all blatant attempts to obtain information about Jack and Sarah and, potentially, to open a pipeline of communication with them.

In one appalling incident, an air charter company from Shannon Airport contacted us to say that someone from the US had tried to hire a plane to fly a banner over the school where the two children were now enrolled. Our local newspaper, *The Limerick Leader*, declined a full-page advertisement from the US with a similar theme.

Support groups were set up for Molly on social media, and multiple images of the children were posted – all without the permission of their guardians. I had to fight tooth and nail with some of the social media giants – a process that is as frustrating as it is exhausting – to have those images removed. Some of the material posted online about Jason was truly vile.

What I am trying to explain is that my grief became extremely complicated in the weeks, months and years after Jason was killed. I didn't realise it at the time, but while I shed tears at Jason's Requiem Mass and felt broken at his graveside,

I hadn't actually been allowed the time or space to grieve. On a physical level, I had said goodbye to my beloved brother. But on an emotional level, I couldn't properly commence the grieving process because of the impending murder trial in the US. It was as if my emotions had been placed on hold. Until justice was found for Jason, I couldn't even attempt to begin to seek closure.

The last thing my brother ever posted on social media was a brief Facebook message that read: 'People will question all the good things they hear about you but believe all the bad without a second thought.' It was posted at 11.15 p.m. on 31 July 2015 – just 36 hours before his murder. I later discovered it was posted after Molly had humiliated him about his weight at a party in front of all their neighbours.

Too late, I realised that Molly had been waging a campaign since June 2011 for Jason to sign adoption papers giving her equal rights to his two children. Jason, mindful of Molly's mental health history, had steadfastly refused – even when Tom Martens had got involved. Had we known what was going on, we would have demanded that Jason immediately bring Jack and Sarah home to Ireland.

The facts that slowly came to light about Molly revealed a deeply troubled young woman who believed children offered her a way of escaping the problems in her life. To my horror, I realised that Jason was simply a means to an end for Molly – she wanted his children, not him. My brother – exhausted from trying to make a doomed marriage work in North Carolina – was in the process of bringing his children back to Ireland. He was killed by Molly and Tom Martens before he could do so.

Davidson County Police quickly got a clearer picture of what was involved. Neighbours revealed a darker side to Molly – of lies, manipulation and bizarre behaviour. Some of Jason's neighbours were so wary of Molly and her fantasies that they didn't want to be left alone with her. Molly had concocted a volume of lies about Jason to the police, which included such outrageous suggestions as him being a mixed martial arts fighter and somehow associated with a paramilitary group in Ireland.

It also emerged that Molly was spending her way through vast quantities of cash. She didn't work, and it was Jason who had entirely funded the €370,000 ($400,000) purchase of their Panther Creek Court home. He had also given Molly €75,000 ($80,000) to furnish the house as she wanted, and had bought her a Honda Pilot. But the spending had reached such a level that Jason had to intervene and try to persuade Molly to adhere to a spending plan. Yet in the year before Jason's murder, Molly spent almost $90,000 – the majority of it on clothing, meals and socialising. We also later discovered that Jason's US life insurance policy had been mysteriously changed online in the months before his killing to exclude his two children – leaving Molly as the only beneficiary.

Just weeks after Molly married my brother in June 2011, she had gone to a divorce lawyer to determine her rights to his children. When informed she had no legal rights to them, Jason was subjected to the unrelenting campaign to grant her legal adoption, which was supported by her father. In a painfully awkward exchange, Tom tried to persuade my brother that the perfect birthday present for Molly would be for him to sign the adoption papers – and Tom even offered to pay the legal fees involved. Jason ignored the proposal.

When categorically disproved, Molly's avalanche of lies made detectives ever more suspicious of her and the circumstances around what had happened that night. The post-mortem examination revealed my brother had been savagely beaten by a concrete paving slab and the metal baseball bat. He was struck so many times on the skull that the pathologist could not accurately count the number of blows. When the block was lifted from the bedroom floor by forensics officers, it left its outline in blood on the carpet.

Incredibly, despite Tom and Molly claiming they had fought for their lives against my brother, they were totally uninjured at the scene. They hadn't suffered a cut, a scratch or a bruise – despite the fact my brother was a strong, heavy man, and Tom was a pensioner. Molly had been wearing a delicate bracelet throughout the incident, and it wasn't bent or damaged. What detectives did have to do at the scene that night was repeatedly warn Molly to stop rubbing her neck in an apparent attempt to create a mark.

From the outset, I believed that Jason had been murdered. But the more I learned about what had happened that night, the more I became absolutely convinced that Tom and Molly had carefully planned my brother's killing. I devoted every second of my time to supporting the Davidson County Police with their investigation, but, argue as I did that the father and daughter had acted with intent, the charges that were finally levelled against them on 4 January 2016 were second-degree murder and voluntary manslaughter. Prosecutors felt there just wasn't enough evidence to prove intent to a jury, which was a prerequisite for a first-degree murder charge. In North Carolina, a first-degree murder conviction can carry the death penalty.

The next 18 months were like being trapped in limbo. We couldn't move on with our lives, we couldn't properly grieve for Jason and the only consolation we had was caring for Jack and Sarah. Seeing them settle back in Limerick and then, slowly but surely, begin to recover and heal after their ordeal was a balm to my wounded soul. At a dark time, it was the only chink of light for us.

On Monday, 17 July 2017 the second-degree murder trial opened before Judge David Lee at Davidson County Superior Court in Lexington, a small city that had once boasted a major furniture manufacturing trade. We travelled over to

North Carolina the previous week to help get acclimated to the scorching heat of a southern US summer. Jason's old friends and workmates had gone out of their way to make us feel welcome, and that helped enormously.

Despite all of the briefings from North Carolina prosecutors, nothing prepared us for the trial itself. We knew that a conviction in North Carolina required a unanimous verdict – if even one of the 12 jurors failed to agree, it would be a hung jury. North Carolina, unlike Ireland, does not allow for majority verdicts. To allow for this, the effort put into jury selection was remarkable, and something we had not expected.

Almost 150 jurors were summoned, and each juror was asked to complete a special 16-page questionnaire. This queried their views on violent crime, the police, Ireland and their own personal histories. It wasn't until the following week, 25 July, that the trial began to hear evidence.

For three weeks, I fought to maintain control as the brutal circumstances of my brother's death were laid bare for the world to see. The people who killed him sat just metres away from me, acting as if nothing out of the ordinary had happened. I once spotted Tom and Molly smiling and happily chatting. My worst day was when the pathology evidence was dealt with. Prosecutors had tried to prepare us for what was coming, but nothing could desensitise us to the image of my brother's blood-soaked, broken body lying on the bedroom floor.

It was so graphic, so shocking that one of the jurors immediately got sick at the sight of the images projected onto the courtroom wall. A total of 12 images were displayed, and only a few of us knew that the very worst images were not displayed at all. One of those unseen photographs still haunts my nightmares. I had dreaded that day, and I wept that evening for my brother, sickened by the cruelty of his death and the indignity shown to him. But I knew that the images were a critical part of countering the lies levelled by Molly and Tom about the true events of that evening.

The forensic evidence tabled by the prosecution was, in my opinion, overwhelming and absolutely central to our hopes of a conviction. Lt Frank Young delivered the crime-scene analysis, while blood-spatter evidence was interpreted by Dr Stuart James. In particular, Dr James's detailing of the scene was extraordinary – right to his opinion that the first blow was struck while Jason was asleep in bed. He also opined that Jason was struck while prone and lying helpless on the ground. The pathology evidence had already indicated that my brother was beaten even after he was dead.

As I had always suspected, Molly opted not to offer evidence. I knew her propensity for high emotion, lies, drama and flights of pure fantasy made her the kind of witness that kept defence lawyers awake at night in fear and, in contrast, prosecutors dream of being allowed to interrogate. My inner voice was also correct in leaving me in no doubt that Tom Martens would take the stand.

Tom was nothing if not assured of his own sense of importance. He liked people to know that he had served in the FBI and, having retired, had worked as a security officer for the US Department of Energy. In his own words, he liked to describe it as 'spy versus spy', almost as if he was some kind of American James Bond. I also knew Tom liked to take public credit for events, even for the lavish wedding his daughter demanded in June 2011 in Tennessee, but which Jason ultimately had to pay for with a $45,000 payment to his new father-in-law.

Tom clearly believed the jury would take him at his word about what he claimed happened that night – and seemed to attach inordinate importance to his education, his qualifications as a lawyer and his FBI service. When the facts didn't match his version of events – such as the forensic evidence – he kept referring back to his version of what had happened. In my opinion, there was an arrogance about Tom, and I wondered if it would grate on the jury.

But he was also honest about his feelings towards my brother – clearly disliking him, obviously believing his daughter should divorce Jason and dismissing their relationship as it 'did not look to me like a good marriage'. A workmate of his had spoken of Tom's intense dislike of his Irish son-in-law – even revealing he refused to go on a family holiday to Washington because Jason was there.

The closing arguments were dramatic. The defence tried to portray my brother as some kind of drunken, angry monster whose pretty blonde wife was saved by the actions of her heroic father. But they carefully ignored the forensic facts and the sheer savagery of the attack Jason had been subjected to. I don't think it was lost on the jury that both Tom and Molly were totally uninjured at the scene. The prosecution, for its part, focused on precisely that.

When prosecutor Alan Martin picked up the metal baseball bat and struck a nearby table with it during closing arguments to underline the type of force used in the blows on Jason, I thought the entire courtroom would jump out of their seats with shock. That one moment, for me, underlined to the jury the precise crux of the case – the sharp, echoing impact of the baseball bat on the metal table was in stark contrast to the fact that Tom and Molly were completely uninjured at the scene and wanted the jury to take them at their word for what happened. Jason wasn't there to offer his version of events. But the force of the bat on the table spoke for him.

Shortly after 3.22 p.m. on Tuesday 8 August, the jury were sent out to consider their verdict. While people were careful not to say it within my hearing, I know several feared it would be a hung jury. Others were gently telling us to brace ourselves for several days of agony waiting for the jury to reach their verdict.

Instead, the jury shocked us all by returning with a verdict at 11.25 a.m. the following day. The media attention on the case was by now incredible, and we arrived at court that morning through a throng of journalists, photographers and TV crews.

It seemed like an eternity as we waited for the judge and then the jury to file into the courtroom. Then the jury foreperson had to hand the issue papers to the court clerk, who handed them to the judge. Seconds later, Judge Lee asked the court registrar to read out the verdicts – and I wept as I heard the confirmation that both Molly and Tom were found guilty of second-degree murder.

The next few hours flashed by in a blur of emotion. I delivered a victim impact statement on behalf of my family. I struggled to hold my emotions in check, but I was determined to do so, as I felt I owed it to Jason. A third victim impact statement, which Jack had insisted on writing, was read out by Mr Martin.

My mother's input into the family statement was the hardest to deliver. She spoke of what had been done to her son as being 'inhuman and barbaric'. She described Jason as 'my pride and joy – kind, generous and sensitive'. 'Instead of Jason's warm embrace, I now look at a cold marble headstone in a graveyard.' My mother begged the court to show Molly and Tom Martens the same leniency they had shown her son.

Unlike Ireland, where sentencing hearings can be postponed for weeks and months, Judge Lee dealt with sentencing directly after the convictions were returned. Molly and Tom each received sentences of 20 to 25 years. They were handcuffed almost immediately and given a few minutes with their families before they were brought for transportation to prison.

I had a prepared statement for the media which I delivered outside the courtroom in the searing heat typical of a North Carolina August. Only Dave and a few close family members realised that I had a second prepared statement ready in case the verdict went in favour of Molly and Tom Martens.

We had been advised to make a statement given the profile that the case had attracted, both in the US and in Ireland. Delivering it wasn't easy, and I drew on all the strength of my coping strategies and counselling sessions because I wanted it to be word perfect for Jason and for my parents.

> We trusted the jury to understand that on 2 August 2015 my niece and nephew were made orphans in a brutal and merciless killing. My parents lost their child, and we all lost the most wonderful brother and friend.
>
> Jason was unarmed, he was struck while he was lying down in the middle of the night, two people battered him until he was dead. Then they battered him again.
>
> When we sat there and listened to the evidence we found [what happened] to be so unbelievable. Who

keeps a brick on their nightstand? We worried that the jury might not find the two accused guilty. But they did, and we thank them for it. I can promise the jury that we will now fulfil our duty to help create a good future for Jason's two children, whom we love so dearly.

I can also promise you that our family is going to stick up for Jason's memory – that this was a good man. Jason was a loving man and he was a great father. You can be sure that Jason Corbett's family will make sure he is remembered for what he was and not for how he died. We would again like to extend our thanks to the people of North Carolina and our supporters in Limerick.

Afterwards, I was ushered through the crowd of reporters by Dave, my siblings and our friends. It was only when we got back to our hotel that I was able to exhale and say a silent prayer that it was all over. And it wasn't until the following day that I realised that photos were taken of the father and daughter as they were led, in prison jumpsuits, from the courthouse to the waiting prison van in shackles.

The days after the conviction and sentencing went by in a blur. The overwhelming feeling we all had was that we just wanted to go home. We were exhausted after more than five weeks in North Carolina, and just wanted to be reunited with Dean, Adam, Jack and Sarah, as well as our extended family back in Limerick. Any relief I felt at the verdict was quickly replaced by the realisation that, no matter what happened in the court, Jason was gone. I would never embrace, laugh with or seek comfort from my brother again.

Over those days, the photographs of Molly and Tom Martens leaving the courthouse dominated the US and Irish newspapers. I took no comfort from the images. This wasn't any vengeance or retribution. It was about justice.

REMINDER

There are far more good people in the world than those whose evil deeds inflict pain and suffering. Sometimes it is important to remind ourselves of that fact when we feel besieged by negative emotions and headlines.

5

IT IS OK TO ASK FOR HELP

The two-year criminal process around Jason's death had, by necessity, forced one thing on me. I hadn't been able to properly grieve for my brother, swamped first by the custody battle over Jack and Sarah and then the relentless effort to support US prosecutors as they prepared their case against Molly and Tom Martens. I simply didn't have the time, and almost every day seemed to bring a new US-related issue to deal with.

We had almost a dozen trips to the US between August 2015 and August 2017, some relating to Jason's estate and others over critical issues relating to the preparation of the prosecution case. That didn't even take into account all the work we had to do from Ireland to refute the many lies being generated by the father and daughter over the type of person Jason was.

In addition to the criminal process over Jason's death, we also had to deal with civil legal issues concerning my brother's estate. We wanted to protect as much as possible of the estate for Jack and Sarah, but, once again, Molly and her family fought us every single step of the way. It was draining, and I wondered if we would ever emerge from the strain of it all.

Unlike with the tragedy over Mags's death, I now had at least some of the tools to handle the tidal wave of emotions that I knew were waiting for me once the fallout from the trial receded and I found myself with time on my hands back in Limerick. But, if I'm honest, I dreaded the quiet times, when the enormity of what happened would finally hit home.

My choice was simple: fight or flight. Face the challenge or run a mile and live forever with the guilt of never being my best self for Jason. I had made a firm promise to him that I would raise his kids and see that they wanted for nothing. I had also spent so much time working for others – now I needed to work to help my family recover from the ordeal. Realising that Dave, Dean, Adam, Jack and Sarah needed me was a major incentive to focus.

They depended on me, and deserved the real Tracey in their lives. There was no way I was going back to the shell of a person I was reduced to in the dark depression after Mags's death. Ignoring my grief over Jason was simply not an option. If I'm honest, I dreaded what I faced – hard as it may seem to understand, but the gruelling US trial process was a kind of escape from my emotions. I had no choice but to park them during the build-up to the trial and then the hearing itself. Jason had been dead for two years, and it was only at this point that I was being allowed time to mourn him and work my way through the emotions over his loss.

The day I began this process was 20 August 2017, as I prepared to board a flight home to Ireland from North Carolina. We were all shattered – emotionally and physically exhausted from the trial process. The strain had been incredible for the past two months. Even the two Irish journalists who had reported on the North Carolina trial since it opened fell ill when they returned home, so draining was the process.

Yet, despite the strain and exhaustion, it had all been worthwhile. We had seen justice done for Jason, and could begin the mourning process knowing we had honoured his life. That was at least one positive, constructive thing to hold onto.

My first step was to shed some of the baggage and take control of my own life and healing. I stuck to my well-being plan, and the very first thing I decided to do was to take action to protect my health. I decided it was time to quit smoking.

I stood at the North Carolina airport and smoked my last cigarette, looking deliberately at the ground as I stubbed it out. I knew it was the right thing to do, and I also felt the timing was opportune. If I was going to be the best version of me possible, kicking my smoking habit was a good start. In one way, it was a symbol of the positive future I wanted, and a gesture towards leaving the toxic habits of the past behind.

Smoking was a crutch, something I could lean on in moments of stress and crisis. It never once crossed my mind to quit in the aftermath of Mags's death and the counselling programme I was undergoing. The simple reason was that I was taking baby steps in my recovery, and it was, to use the World War II phrase, 'a bridge too far' for me at that time. I wasn't ready, and I hate to admit it, but smoking was one of the things that helped me cope back then.

But it was different now. Quitting the habit was, I felt, a clear commitment to recovery, health and well-being. If I was going to devote myself to my family, this was a positive step I could take to help myself. The best way I can explain it was that I was now putting myself firmly in the driving seat of my life.

Over the coming weeks and months, I did have pangs of longing for a cigarette, particularly in certain circumstances, such as after a cup of coffee, or when I was feeling particularly stressed. All former smokers will relate when I mention that moment when you enjoy that first cigarette in the day. The time you look forward to the most. I used to walk the grounds of the organisation I worked at to process the last meeting and prepare for the next, and to check in with the groundsmen and staff. I found it such a challenge to do it without lighting up.

Thankfully, I didn't crack – I stayed off cigarettes, because I had learned other, better means of coping. When I arrived home to Ireland, I had four children to greet, love and support me. In turn, I had to support them. Protecting my health was one of the most practical things I could do for all of us.

The welcome we received on arriving home was the warmest and most comforting I have ever felt. Having the children's arms wrapped around me was like a safety blanket, an unspoken reassurance that everything would be alright. We took a week away together in a warmer climate, and turned off our phones and had no TVs. Together, we had seven days of readjusting, getting over jet lag and sitting down together to dinner each evening.

The kids had so much to say, and were beyond happy to have us home. Dave and I were frazzled and slightly bewildered after our experience, so it gave us time in privacy to be together, safely away from any media. We told no one where we were – only my mother and sister and two close friends.

When we returned, we set aside more family time, went out for a few meals and met close friends who had supported us throughout the nightmare of the previous two years. Once again I was reminded of the importance of family and sticking close to the good people in your life. We drew strength from each other, and that was precisely what I needed in August 2017.

My employers had been great to give me the time off, yet I was the chief executive and they expected me on return to be present and to catch up on everything that had piled up from late July when I left for the US. It wasn't easy. I had come back a very different person who had been deeply affected by my experience.

As I tried to resume my old life, self-doubt began to hover around me. After all we had gone through, the details of ordinary working life seemed so trivial. One day I'm listening to the pathology details of how my brother was beaten to death, and three weeks later I'm trying to deal with business plans, spreadsheets and work rosters.

There were times it all seemed so utterly meaningless. Why are people working? Why are they asking me stupid questions? I struggled to put myself firmly in the 'now'. I dug deep and did my duty as an employee but, if I'm honest, my priorities at that time were elsewhere.

It was the same with friends. They tried to help by taking my mind off what had happened in the US. They'd invite me for dinner or drinks and carefully keep the discussion firmly on issues such as family, shopping, local news, holidays and sport. Any mention of North Carolina and Jason was studiously avoided.

I knew they were only trying to help and doing their best to cope with an awful situation. They were trying to support a friend in need. But a part of my brain also wanted to scream 'stop' at the latest story about a beautiful dress bought for a bargain price in a particular Adare boutique, queries about my absence from book club or why I'd cancelled arrangements to meet for dinner and drinks. These were all things I had loved to do in the past. I just felt like I was allergic to them.

The angry part of me wanted to tell them all to fuck off with their perfect lives. Did they have any idea what the pain was like? What I had just gone through with my family? Did they really think a story about a cheap dress or a great new restaurant was going to help me fill the gaping void left by Jason's murder?

I was struggling to reconnect with the world around me, and what I really struggled with were what I called my 'sliding doors moments'. These were the times when I focused on inconsequential moments that might have changed the entire trajectory of not just my life but potentially that of Jason and the children. I was tormented by 'what ifs'. If I had reacted differently, might things have turned out differently? Why hadn't I picked up on the signals that there was something going on with Molly?

Jason had raised doubts about leaving Ireland to me. Selfishly, I wanted him to stay, but I put those feelings aside and tried to look at it from Jason's point of view. Having benefited so much from counselling, I advised him to go the same route. I even booked him a few sessions, which he later said had helped him. If I hadn't done that, would he have stayed in Limerick and declined to move to the US, staying close by his family support network? If I had told him I'd be desperately lonely without him, would he have made a different decision?

Jason had called me a few weeks before his murder, but I had missed the call. I had called him back and his phone had gone to voicemail. Normally, I rarely left messages, and would instead ring back. But something just prompted me, and I said something like, 'Hey J, give me a call. We were just talking about the fact that you are now at the four years point, where we said you'd be back home. We all love and miss you. Isn't it time you came back home to us?'

He called the house phone the next evening. I was in the bath, so Dave took the call. That was the call where Jason admitted to Dave that he was coming back to Ireland. What if I had taken that call? Would he have confided in me? Almost certainly. Would the timeline have changed? Would he have acted more cautiously with his travel plans if he had spoken to me? If he told me about Molly's bizarre behaviour, would I have urged him to be more careful? I would have most likely caught the next flight over.

There were a thousand 'what ifs' rattling through my mind. By engaging with them, I forgot the cardinal rule of my counselling sessions – that I am powerless to change the past. I can learn from the past to improve my present, but I can't change things. Accepting that fact is a core pillar of recovery. But it is much easier said than done, and I continue to work on this.

But such were the emotions and stresses before, during and after the North Carolina trial, that my GP was concerned I was close to burn-out, both physically and emotionally. I had endured the trauma of the six-week trial process in the US largely on adrenalin, but now my system was crashing back to earth.

One day, I collapsed in my bedroom and Dave had to call for an ambulance. I didn't want to worry anyone, but it seemed my body had very different ideas. I spent a week in the hospital with endocrine issues and high cortisol levels. The nervous system is the command centre of the body and is responsible for how you experience your environment. It's a little like a highway running through your entire body connecting nerves, muscles and cells, and sending messages between them. When it's regulated, we feel present, calm, well. Think of the fight-or-flight feeling you get if you hear a sudden noise – you jump but your body goes back into a regulated state. When it doesn't revert, you can feel overwhelmed, anxious, numb, sleepy, angry, or depressed, and sometimes you can get stuck there. When we get stuck we don't feel present or connected. An amazingly simple thing I do to regulate my nervous system is to control my breathing. It really helps to soothe the body and mind. Just get comfortable and breathe in for a count of four and out for a count of eight. The slow exhale reminds your body you are safe.

I began to realise that if I wasn't careful, my system crashes wouldn't have soft landings. Even with the success of my ongoing counselling support, my doctor felt I could benefit from even more expert help.

Each day seemed to bring its own variety of aches and pains. In a way, they were a physical symptom of grief. I had back pain, joint pain, headaches and stiffness. My doctor once explained that the pain could be caused by the overwhelming amount of stress hormones being released during the grieving process. These effectively stun the muscles they contact. I was a physical wreck from 2015 to 2017 – I had no time for self-care, and was compartmentalising and storing up this mountain of grief and trauma.

Running on 'high alert' constantly drained my energy and I felt exhausted most evenings. I was getting through less and less work but felt more and more tired. Dave recognised I wasn't myself and urged me to see the doctor, fearing I had picked up some kind of bug or infection. The entire family knew there was something not right.

To add fuel to the fire, I suddenly found myself struggling to sleep. I would climb into bed totally wrecked from the day, feeling low from poor diet, lack of exercise and overwork, only to lay staring at the ceiling, unable to find some desperately sought-after sleep. It was wearing me down.

During the day, my mind seemed overwhelmed and foggy. I wasn't able to concentrate or do anything productive. It was as if my body was a car with the handbrake engaged and stuck in second gear, unable to go faster even though my foot was to the floor on the accelerator. The harder I tried to focus, the worse it got. The more frustrated I became over my ability to engage 'the real me', the less I was able to achieve.

The net result was that, from being a person who thrived on being around others and closely networking with other people, I started to self-isolate. It was the only way I thought I could cope given how poorly I felt. Simply the idea of being around other people made me uncomfortable. There is no such word but, at that point in time, the world just felt too 'peopley' for me. I didn't know how to handle the normal gossip, jokes, laughter and social planning that came with being in the world.

I was wracked with fear and anxiety. Despite knowing I was surrounded by decent, kind-hearted and caring people, I was terrified of allowing the barriers down so they could see just how bad I really felt. It was a toxic mixture of pride, anxiety and lack of confidence. I was so unwell I truly felt other people's happiness jarred with me. It upset my rhythm of misery.

In the workplace, I was known as hard-working, goal-orientated and confident Tracey. Inside, I felt only a shell of the person I once was. The trouble was I had no idea how to find my way back to being that person, the old me. I was lost, and had no map back to the safety of my true self.

I was feeling very despondent, and didn't know where to turn next. The end of the trial had also brought a lot of emotions back into focus – things I had happily kicked down the road while the trial was ongoing over the past two years.

My doctor quietly suggested I have a chat with a clinical psychiatrist just to get an expert opinion on exactly where I stood. He was also very aware of the complex nature of our experience, and was of course our family physician. He was not only Jack and Sarah's doctor but had also been the GP for Jason. Our doctor is a very compassionate man, and took a pragmatic view of it. He basically asked me, what did I have to lose? With no other options, I somewhat reluctantly agreed and attended my first session a couple of weeks later.

The clinical psychiatrist was astute, matter-of-fact and razor-sharp. Our first meeting involved her firing questions incessantly at me. I was questioned so extensively that I didn't have time to think, which was incredibly important – I didn't have a chance to frame defensive answers or steer her away from the truth. It was relentless.

For the best part of an hour, I said things I had never uttered before, things I had absolutely no intention of ever speaking about to any other human being. There was no filter, no premeditated answers – simply the truth about how I felt and where I believed my life was.

Having listened to what I had to say, she quickly assessed that grief wasn't my only issue. True, I was devastated by Mags's and Jason's deaths. But she suggested my problems were compounded by the fact that I was a people-pleaser – I was trying to fix everything for everyone, not just for myself. I was trying to put my arms around the world, and was slowly destroying myself in the process.

The harder I tried to perform the impossible, the more frustrated and anxious I became – and the less I was able to do as a result. I was exhausted, and yet wouldn't release the weights that were dragging me down. Her view was that I had some 'toxic' people in my life who weren't doing me any favours. By this, she meant people who didn't have my best interests at heart and still had an overly powerful influence on me. It wasn't that they were out to do me harm. It was simply that they put their selfish interests before what was good for me – and the result was toxic. In a way, they projected their problems onto me – and I had willingly added them to my own burden.

I had distanced myself from some as a result of my counselling sessions. But others still had a large influence on my life – and who turned to me for a multitude of needs. It was very much a case of: 'Don't worry, Tracey will sort that out' or 'Tracey, can you help with this?'

Since childhood, I had been subtly bullied by a few people. I had allowed it to continue for years, partly to avoid a confrontation and partly because I was afraid of the consequences of tackling it. Above all else, I didn't want to rock the boat. Like most people, I hated the idea of confrontation, so coped as best I could, inadvertently allowing the people-pleasing side of my personality to expand to dangerous proportions. The problem was, in the wake of Mags's and Jason's deaths, and other events in my life, I simply couldn't cope anymore.

It was time for me to learn some harsh lessons. Some people may consider themselves to be our friends but try to exert a right to demand how we live our lives. It is never overt. In almost all cases, it is subtle. But they somehow try to influence our lives through advice, diktats, arrangements and social matters. What is camouflaged as a favour transpires to be a massive benefit for them.

I have no idea what they derived from it. Maybe they thrived on the fear they instilled in others. Perhaps they felt their lives would be better if only everyone else did what they wanted them to do. Perhaps it is a reflection of their own pain they try to project onto you. No matter the reason, each request or demand was followed up by yet another. I could never say 'no' for fear of the potential consequences, thereby becoming the strategic 'enabler' in their lives.

The psychiatrist recommended I engage more regularly with counselling but also that I also consider adopting a mindfulness programme or meditation. She wanted me to focus on myself and where my life was – not on what I should be doing for others.

It is hard to credit, but I only had two sessions with the psychiatrist. She didn't heal me, and there was no silver bullet offered, but, for the first time, I saw the outline of a strategy to help drag my life back into the sunshine. That remarkably perceptive woman, at the conclusion of our second session, simply asked me, 'Isn't it time you said no?'

I had never thought that was an option. Up until that point, I had thought I needed to be a miracle worker, sorting all my own issues as well as taking on the problems of anyone else who asked me. For the first time, I realised it was OK to say that I had enough to cope with on my own, and that I couldn't help carry the burdens of others as well.

I needed to create my own boundaries, put my health and the well-being of my family before all others and, in some cases, put daylight between me and people who weren't good for me. Above all else, I had to make a solemn promise to myself that I would no longer allow myself to be bullied.

There is a time in your life when the stress, pain and anxiety reach breaking point. You can and should ask for help. I realised I had arrived at that stage on my journey. I reached out and was overwhelmed with the support I received from my husband, family, siblings, parents, true friends and healthcare professionals.

That was the turning point – the time when I realised that it was acceptable for me to say I was no longer prepared to accept the negative impact of others on my life and the lives of my family. It was as if the blindfold had fallen off and I saw that some people are so angry, buried so deep in a pit of guilt and blame, that you have no option but to carefully remove yourself from their orbit.

Unconsciously, I had been trying to help drag some people back from their own darkness. All I accomplished was to take on a burden that, combined with my own loss, was simply too great to bear. I slowly realised that while my actions were noble and born out of obligation, my first duty was to myself and my family. Over time, I understood that some of my relationships just weren't healthy for me.

The first step was the hardest, but it was also the simplest. I discovered that if I spoke up for myself, the people involved lost their power over me. Their 'shock and awe power' vanished when I uttered the magic freedom word: 'no'. One of the best phrases I learned was: 'If you have an opinion about how I should live my life, please raise your hand and then put it over your mouth.'

I told a handful of people that I wished them well but that it was important they lived their own lives and allowed me to live mine. For my own welfare, I needed a bit of distance to recover and get my bearings after all that had happened. There were mistakes I had made but they were my mistakes, and I had the right to make them – and to now learn from them.

A few people took my stance badly. When I was no longer following their detailed road map in life, I immediately switched from being an ally to an unwitting opponent. In one case, an individual subjected me to hurtful comments, both in public and in private. Where once we had a good relationship, it broke down almost entirely – simply because I could no longer play the role they wanted me to. When I refused to follow their diktats in life, I suddenly became a target.

While I knew they were also in a dark place of their own through pain and loss – and I had tremendous sympathy for them on a human level – I wasn't going to back down. The more my recovery progressed, the stronger I became in defending my right to live my own life and put the needs of my family first.

It was very hurtful seeing a relationship slide into toxicity when it was the very last thing I wanted. But I learned that, in life, there are times when you have to grant others the right to be wrong.

From this point on, I felt the children had first call on my time, particularly after all that had happened in North Carolina. As a family, we had also been forced to undertake enormous costs in relation to both the fight to protect Jason's estate and the North Carolina prosecution. Keeping our heads above water financially was now a pressing need for both Dave and myself.

Counselling had taught me to prioritise what was important – and not to rush the recovery process. Everything needed to be dealt with in its own time. Healing would occur over its own timescale. My priority would be to look after myself and my family. In counselling parlance, I had to give time, time.

Grief hadn't just singled me out. My husband, Dave, was devastated by the loss of his brother, Kevin, right in the middle of the build-up to the North Carolina trial. Dave had four siblings: Kevin, Michael and Linda all emigrated in the 1980s when the Irish economy was at its lowest ebb; his youngest brother, Paul, remained in Limerick.

Kevin, Michael and Linda had all secured US green cards and moved across the Atlantic for work. All three were based for a time in Florida, though they remained in close contact with their family back in Limerick. Like the Corbetts, the Lynches were a tight-knit family and utterly devoted to their mother, Norah, who had raised them after the premature death of their father, John.

Kevin had been diagnosed with an aggressive form of cancer and died in 2016. Despite his diagnosis, he had insisted on doing everything he could to help us after 2 August 2015 and during our subsequent trips to North Carolina.

He rallied all those close to him in Florida to share in their support of my family, and was a pillar of strength for us in the first year of our fight for justice for Jason. Kevin's friends became our friends. I loved Kevin dearly, but no more so than when he called regularly with advice and to check in on me.

Like Kevin, Linda was a rock of support. In the week before the trial began in Davidson County, she travelled to North Carolina to show solidarity with us – and brought special 'care packages' for every one of us, each labelled with our names, all aimed at helping make our US stay more comfortable. It was the simplest of gestures, but one I will never forget.

Kevin's death hit Dave really hard. It wasn't just that Kevin was so young; it was the speed with which cancer claimed him. He was the first of the siblings to die, and it reminded Dave of previous shock losses, such as the death of his parents.

I know now that Dave felt he had to remain strong for me and the family, because we were about to enter the critical build-up to the trial, and he was the lynchpin of our family. I wasn't the only one dealing with delayed grief. Without his support, I simply would not have been able to go on.

Back in Ireland, I visited Jason and Mags's grave. Almost every time I went to the Castlemungret Cemetery, I broke down. It was all too painful, too overwhelming. Everything about the plot brought me to tears – particularly the sight of the mementoes that Jack and Sarah had left over the years for their lost parents.

Standing at the grave, I told Jason I had kept my vow to him. The children were now safe in his beloved Limerick, and they would be raised surrounded by a sea of love. The two people who had betrayed his trust and taken his life were both now behind bars and facing 20 to 25 years for their heinous crime.

Going to the cemetery offered some comfort, but it was very raw. I needed another way to work through my grief. Having made so many mistakes in terms of my handling of emotions after Mags's death, I had learned not to shut others out, and to ask for help if I felt I needed it.

Over the weeks immediately after our return to Limerick, I asked friends what they would suggest. Several said that if visiting the grave was so painful, why not write out my feelings and memories, almost like a note from the heart to Jason?

The idea somehow felt right, and perfectly suited to me. I was an organised person who lived daily life by schedules and plans. So why not try to describe in writing the fear, hurt, anger, betrayal and loss I had endured over the past few years? Not to mention recording in detail all the things I loved and missed most about Jason.

Writing became a form of therapy for me. It was as if I was communicating directly to Jason, explaining what we had done, why we had done it and what we had planned for his children. Nothing was too trivial to write – funny childhood memories that a passing incident had brought back to mind, a wave of sadness sparked by hearing a song on the radio that Jason used to love to sing, or my fears about what the future might hold.

Often, I would simply describe events in my life to Jason – what had happened that day, what was going on in the children's lives, what family news I had and even bits of gossip from Limerick, Raheen and Janesboro. Here are a few examples of what I wrote:

March 2018 – J you are not going to believe this! You will be both shocked and delighted … Paul is a daddy! I know!! It's been months since Simone gave birth to Elena but I have to share it with you, watching him parenting her would make you proud. She is the apple of his eye.

December 2018 – You are going to be well jealous that we are going to the Pro Am with the kids. We bought them for friends and each other as a Christmas gift. When Luke got it, he was looking at it confused … lol. BTW I put away your golf clubs for when Jack is older, I cleaned them carefully, had a little cry and stored them in the attic alongside the ones you had got for him. He has grown so much they are too small for him now but he will get to play with your clubs someday soon.

Hi J – We stopped doing the panto last year. It was another ruthless step in healing. We had so many wonderful years together. I miss every one of them and I miss you and Mags. Millennium in Mam and Dads will still remain one of our epic nights of laughter. Life didn't end that night as everyone was joking. It's taken me time to learn it hasn't ended after your deaths either. It is very different, though we still do the takeout curry tradition on December 23. Jack says that's his night to host us all when he is older and he will carry on the curry tradition. He always goes for the quirky option. You are both always in our hearts.

I wondered whether my lost twin was somehow guiding my hand as a jumble of memories and emotions spilled from my pen – helping me to communicate with the spirit of the person I had depended so much on in life. Without realising it at the time, I was drawing comfort from the discovery of a connection with my lost brother that was as personal as it was secure.

A lot of my writing was inspired by the things I had discovered about Jason's own life during the North Carolina trial process. I had been given access to all of Jason's private documents, as well as his emails. Some – particularly those involving his adored children – brought a smile to my face. Jason's immense pride in Jack and Sarah was clear from everything he ever wrote about them.

Other items made for very difficult reading, particularly the messages he had written to Molly. It was clear that Jason had deep concerns over the relationship – and yet had clearly fallen for this young American woman. But Molly's replies were always imploring, always begging him not to turn his back on a second chance at love and to fully commit to a relationship with her.

Having to read how someone was lied to, deceived and essentially led down a road that ended in their violent death in the most sickening of circumstances was appalling. With every fibre of my being I wanted to scream a warning to my brother through the laptop or the written page. But I was powerless to change the past. Accepting that became a major part of my recovery process.

Arguably, the biggest single benefit for me was that writing allowed me to process and order my emotions. For instance, there might be a day where emotions would whirl around my mind – fury at Molly for what she and her father had done to Jason and my family. Or maybe anger at God for having allowed such evil things to happen to good people. Somehow, putting those emotions down on paper helped expel them, or at the very least, partially defuse them.

They were less corrosive on a piece of paper after I had written them down, as though I had captured them rather than allowing them to continue to swirl around my brain. By writing them down, I also gave them order – the anger and fear slowly turned to determination and courage.

Seeing the emotions in black and white helped me to focus on what was really important – working to see justice done for my brother, supporting my family and embracing the remarkable solidarity being shown to us by ordinary people.

The most painful part of recovery is having to face up to and deal with your emotions. Yet the most rewarding part of recovery is finding a way to do just that. I found my own path to recovery – and it involved turning my emotions around, swapping out anger, fear and hatred for courage, love, compassion and empathy.

It dawned on me, as part of the writing process, that I had a choice. I could drown in negative emotions that would eat away at my spirit like acid, or I could focus on love, courage and solidarity – the things that would help ease my pain and prepare me for my new future. I chose not to allow the fallout from evil to damage my future.

It was one of the most powerful discoveries I have ever made: that love never stops. It can't be beaten to death or destroyed by lies. My love for my brother, for Mags and others never once faltered, not even in my darkest moments. When I realised the extent of the love and compassion being shown to our family at a time of our greatest need, I drew strength from it.

There were tough times. I found Christmas particularly difficult, because it brought back so many reminders of Jason,

Mags, Norah, Kevin and others. Christmas had always been a very special time in our house – and Jason was at the root of so many of my favourite festive memories, both as a child and as an adult.

As children, we would sit by the blazing fire with our Santa gifts, crackers sitting on the dinner table and all of us excited about some Christmas film on the TV. Jason loved Christmas, and as an adult he never really lost his inner child.

It was on Christmas morning that Dave and I asked Jason and Mags to be godparents for our yet-to-be-born son, Adam. Mags was so touched that she cried with happiness. During Christmas 2006, our first without Mags, Dave's mother Norah was tireless in her efforts to offer some festive cheer to our heartbroken household. Just 12 months later, it was Jason's turn to try to return the favour with Dave, who had just lost his mother.

Before long, my writings came to form a kind of biography of my brother. It was very much the language of the heart – who Jason was, what he meant to us and how a part of him was still with us thanks to cherished memories. I realised that, by committing the memories to paper, I ensured they would not be forgotten – and that they would serve as a well of information for Jack and Sarah about who their father really was.

A friend said the writings deserved to be published in the form of a book about our experiences. Initially, I dismissed the idea. Writing about Jason had initially been a means of therapy, a way of expressing my grief and working through the pain. It had been intended to be a very private experience.

But, the more I thought about it, I began to realise that it was the perfect way to honour Jason's memory and counter the character assassination that Molly and Tom Martens had engaged in as part of their desperate bid to save their own skins. One of the worst parts of the entire trial experience was the vile lies told about my brother, many of which had been quoted in the media.

Some family members, including my parents, Marilyn and Wayne, enthusiastically endorsed the idea of a book. Other family members weren't so sure and argued that it was best to let the dust settle on all that had happened. Friends were very supportive, and many said a book would be entirely in keeping with the entire concept of the 'Justice for Jason' campaign.

Over time, I realised that we would never be allowed peace, with the Martens' appeal against their conviction and sentence already signalled for the North Carolina Court of Appeals. Horrific material was also being posted about Jason online and, worst of all, Molly and Tom had granted interviews with a US TV network before their trial. This was then broadcast after they had been jailed. Needless to say, Jason was portrayed as some kind of drunken Irish brute.

It dawned on me that their lies would never stop until they either ran out of appeal avenues or won their freedom. It was a key factor in persuading me to agree to write a book to defend my brother's good name and set the public record straight.

My Brother Jason was published by Gill Books in May 2018 and, to my enormous surprise and pride, went to No. 1 on the bestsellers chart. I was overwhelmed with messages of support from across Ireland, Europe and the US. Some of the messages from the US were particularly inspirational, coming from people who had followed the North Carolina trial process. Needless to say, there were a few negative comments. But I was now strong enough and confident enough to dismiss them.

Writing the book had brought back so many memories of Jason. From childhood escapades I had all but forgotten about right through to hilarious stories about him at work or socialising with his friends in Limerick and North Carolina.

One unexpected benefit of the book was the number of stories that people shared with us about Jason, many of which we had never heard before. From his kindness to Irish immigrants arriving in North Carolina through to his fierce loyalty to his friends and workmates.

Each story was an affirmation of the good person that Jason was. It was a very gentle reminder to me that, when we are at our lowest ebb, simply asking for help or contact from another person can yield unexpected benefits. If I hadn't been open to the idea of writing about the death of my brother, I would never have learned half the things I did about him. One young Irish couple contacted me to explain how they had met Jason shortly after their arrival in North Carolina – which, unlike New York and Boston, is not a major Irish immigrant centre – and he had offered them invaluable advice about work, socialising and healthcare.

Many of the manuscript pages ended up tear-stained as I relived both the happy and sad memories. When I was 40, Jason secretly flew back to Limerick from North Carolina just to surprise me. Of all the presents I got that day, the bear hug from Jason – grinning at how thrilled I was just to see him – was the very best. It was the finest surprise present I ever received, and it helped make that weekend the best of my life.

I cried recalling that incident, but they were tears of pride as I realised my baby brother thought so much of me that he was willing to fly halfway across the world just to surprise me at my birthday party.

Publishing the book involved a large number of TV and radio interviews and, contrary to what you might have thought, these actually helped me with the grieving process. I was able to speak openly about Jason, describe the kind of person he was and outline the pain and suffering my family had gone through since his murder.

Every time I spoke about Jason, I felt a little bit better afterwards. In particular, I recall one interview I did with Lynn

– who was best friends with Jason and Mags – on Live95FM with Joe Nash. The interview was about an hour long, and it ended up being like reminiscences between friends.

It was as though speaking about Jason kept the memory of him alive. Before each interview I felt nervous and anxious but, within a few seconds of beginning to speak, I felt a confidence surge through me – as if I was fulfilling my vow to my brother.

One of the most remarkable experiences was doing a reading at a literary festival in Trim, Co. Meath. I was invited to read from *My Brother Jason* at the Hinterland Festival and then take part in a questions and answers session about the book and the US trial. There was once a time when I would have been convinced that never in a million years would I have been able to go through such an experience. But I did. The hall was packed, and yet my voice never faltered as I spoke about what an incredible person my brother was.

Afterwards, I was taken aback when a queue formed at the back of the hall. I turned and asked what it was for, only to be told it was people who wanted to meet me. They wanted a book autographed, to wish me and my family well or to share a story of their own about loss. It filled my heart with a mixture of pride and joy to realise just how much support and empathy is out there if we can only tap into it. It was a very special day for me.

A close friend has a motto that there are far more good people in life than bad people, if you only give them a chance. Sometimes, we have to experience support in our lives to realise that this is true. For every nasty comment I received about the book or my brother, I received one hundred supportive comments and messages of solidarity about how others who had lost loved ones in similar circumstances and yet somehow drew strength from what I had written. On its own, that made the entire project worthwhile.

It was also a salutary reminder to me that I wasn't the only person dealing with deep, bitter grief in my life. The 'Justice for Jason' page had introduced me to the fact that there were hundreds and thousands of people mourning loved ones, many lost to violent crime.

Worse still, many had never seen justice done for their loved ones, and this was a constant, aching pain in their lives. Some simply tried to cope by reaching out to help others. By showing solidarity with someone else in pain, you can forget your own grief for a time. That was probably the biggest lesson I drew from my book experience.

I discovered that people want to attach some kind of meaning to their loss. Both from the 'Justice for Jason' campaign page and my book, I realised that people draw comfort from speaking out about their loss, their pain – if they believe it can help others and, perhaps, ensure a similar tragedy is avoided.

My book took that discovery to an entirely new level. I received heart-warming letters from people who had lost loved ones in similar situations. Cards arrived from people across the world who said they were inspired by the courage our family had shown. Many wrote to say that, though they had never met Jason, they felt, having read the book, as if they had known him. Others wrote that they had lost figures just like Jason in their own lives. The number of letters I received from people in the US was nothing short of astonishing.

Some people were kind enough to send Mass cards, memorial tributes or even spiritual tokens. Others simply wrote to say they had gone to their local church, mosque or synagogue to say a prayer and light a candle for Jason and for our family.

Words cannot convey how powerful those messages were for us. There is nothing more comforting on this earth than the feeling of human solidarity. The thought that people would take the time to reach out to us – sometimes from the other side of the world – to wish us well and to express their support for our family was enormously uplifting.

I was beyond moved by the messages. In truth, they were overwhelming. I drew such strength from them that saying 'thank you' simply didn't cover what I had received from all these strangers. Writing the book had involved opening myself up to strangers – and, in turn, strangers had opened themselves up to me about the tragedies in their own lives.

I don't know how I would have coped with Jason's loss but for the legacy of my counselling and the therapeutic impact of the book. Without realising it, I was working through my memories, emotions and anxieties and emerging a stronger, wiser and more focused person. I had dropped my defensive barriers and opened myself up to support from others.

Not everyone will publish a book to help them with their grief. Most people won't want to. But I can highly recommend the practice of writing down your feelings, about both your loss and the loved one involved. I found it helped me work my way through my emotions and my fears. It gave a purpose and direction to sorting through my memories. There were days I was too upset to write anything. Then there were other days, when my hand started to cramp from writing out golden memories, some of which had me laughing out loud.

My experience is that writing out your feelings and memories helps you negotiate your way through the maze of emotions to your end goal of perspective and acceptance. An idea that you just can't formulate in your mind can suddenly become clearer and easier to accept when put down on paper, when you see it in black and white.

One friend had an aversion to writing memories on paper or slowly typing them out on a computer keyboard. So they came up with the idea of meticulously recording their memories using a Dictaphone. The memories were then carefully dated. The system worked fine for them. And that is the point – use whatever means suits you to deal with those memories and sort through the emotions surrounding your grief.

Your loved one may be departed, but they are not really gone. After all, if you are writing out cherished recollections you had with them, they are still very much alive in your memory. Those memories are always there when you need them most. If you hold a legacy of love for someone in your heart and in your memory, surely they cannot truly be gone?

I also began to realise that the fact that Jason had lived was far more important than the fact that he was gone. He had touched so many lives in his 39 years, and it was something that made me very proud as his sister and friend. My brother had lived his life to the full and, while his future had been stolen from him, I refused to allow the legacy of his life work to be hijacked as well. That was something I drew tremendous comfort from.

Another outcome of the process was a renewed appreciation of just how precious life is. I was reminded that every day needed to be embraced and lived to its maximum possible degree. Because we just don't know what lies around the corner. Life is so, so precious, and we get reminders of that all around us.

During the pre-trial process in North Carolina, I was driving with Dave along a main highway when a car suddenly swerved across the lanes in front of us, narrowly missing our car before ploughing directly into a utility pole.

As the dust settled, I saw a little girl get out of the car and bolt into oncoming traffic. Dave pulled our car onto the hard shoulder and I ran to drag the little girl back to the safety of the roadside. I held the sobbing youngster in my arms and she clung to me as we waited for the emergency services to arrive. It transpired that her mother was a diabetic. She had slipped into unconsciousness during an insulin-related incident and was senseless as her car veered out of control and crashed.

We did everything we could at the scene, and I was taken aback to see, once the little girl had calmed down, how brave she was. But what struck me most was how the rest of the world kept going – cars and trucks flashed by, people went about their daily chores, unwilling to be delayed or side-tracked while one family unit went through a traumatic upheaval by the roadside, one that I prayed wouldn't be life-altering. Grief can feel a little like that – the whole world keeps moving while you are in your living nightmare.

And yet while others focused on their own priorities, the emergency services moved heaven and earth to help both the young mother and the little girl at the scene. It was only months later that it dawned on me that there are so many positives and spirit-enhancing incidents in life if we only take the time to consider them and switch our focus away from the negatives. I often wonder about that little girl and her mother and how our paths crossed that day for the briefest of time. It helped me to focus on the world around me.

We have a choice in life – we can look to the heavens in wonder or we can stare at the ground and focus on the mud.

REMINDER

Change can be difficult and challenging – but it is never impossible. Some of the biggest and most transformative changes in our lives can begin with baby steps.

6

MAKE RECOVERY EASIER ON YOURSELF – MIND YOUR MIND, BODY AND SPIRIT

Like a lot of Irish people, I have a strong faith but a complicated relationship with my Church. My faith has acted as an anchor for me in the storms of life. In the darkest days, when I struggled to hold on to some kind of sanity, my faith acted as a beacon for me, guiding me back to safer waters, though it later transformed itself into spirituality and mindfulness.

I was raised a Catholic and received my First Holy Communion and Confirmation. My parents ensured that their children attended Mass each Sunday in Limerick. My mam had very strong faith and was never too far away from prayer books and her beloved Rosary beads throughout her life. Mam firmly believed that promptly christening her children – and her grandchildren – was like a vaccine against sin. She prayed every single day of her life. When we were children, she saw to it that we also prayed each evening – leading us as a family in saying the Rosary in our family home.

Even when my mother's health began to fail and she was physically unable to attend Mass, she would watch Mass on the television or listen to it on the radio and continue with her nightly prayers. Her prayer book had prayers for almost every need her family might have. Her faith was like a comfort blanket to her, and I admired her dedication to it.

Through my family, I became involved in the Legion of Mary and, certainly for the early part of my adult life, attended Mass nearly every week. From my parents, I inherited the conviction that, in life, some type of faith was extremely important. As a child, I attended Mass each Sunday and went to the Legion of Mary on a Tuesday evening. Then there was regular attendance at Confession, and going to church on special occasions and holidays. At the time I never questioned it, because it was what everyone else in my community was doing. It was so normal it went unquestioned.

I regularly went to the Stations of the Cross, which some people call the Way of Sorrows. Station by station, I would move along the periphery of the quiet church, saying prayers at each – if I missed one or felt I didn't do it right I would revisit it. I'm pretty thorough when I do something. Anything worth doing is worth doing well, has always been my motto. I took this approach to my religion.

It so happens that I was named after our local priest's mother, a lovely, kind lady called Theresa Young, who was also our next-door neighbour. She was really a good neighbour to my mam, and so when I was born my mother named me after her. Mrs Young was comforting, kind and friendly. Her own children were Kathleen and Joe. Giving was in her nature. I remember if I was feeling unwell as a young child she would feed me jelly and ice cream, insisting it would help perk me up.

Her son, Joe, became a priest when I was young, and he would often refer to the connection between his mother and myself. He later lived next door to Dave's mam, Norah – before we met each other, coincidentally. Fr Joe married Dave and me. He also christened our kids, and played all the other important roles you would expect from your family priest.

It was Fr Joe who gave me one of the best pieces of life advice I ever received. On the day of our wedding, he turned to Dave and me, warning us that, 'You should never go to sleep on an argument.' That one piece of advice has carried Dave and me through so many difficult years.

But, like a lot of other people, over time I subconsciously began to discern the difference between having to go and wanting to go to Mass. It wasn't as though I made any definite decision not to attend; I simply drifted when I reached my late teens and early 20s. That being said, Mass attendance at major religious celebrations such as Christmas, Easter and

All Saints' Day went unquestioned. Like other Irish people, I also visited the graves of relatives for All Souls, and when my mother wanted to lay a Christmas wreath as a memorial offering.

What I did notice was that I seemed to benefit more from retreats than from ordinary Mass attendance. There was something about a retreat that struck a chord deep within me – the quiet, the focus and the peacefulness. Days after completing a retreat I would have a feeling of calm and serenity about me.

In later years, my church attendance was reduced. At times, it was because I was busy with family life, social commitments or even business. If it sounds indefensible, that's because it is. Finding time for faith and spirituality is a vital part of the human experience, which I had to learn through pain and suffering.

In later years, I didn't go to Mass because I was angry with God. In my eyes, He had allowed terrible things to happen to some of the people I loved most. Like millions of Christians before me, I struggled to reconcile the concept of a loving, caring and kind God with the evil suffered by good people. It just didn't make any sense. How could such suffering be allowed to happen? It seemed so unfair.

After first Mags's death and then Jason's murder, I found myself facing a crisis of faith. My Mass attendance had slowly dwindled even before Jason's death, but after his murder, it largely stopped altogether, except for major ceremonies.

This wasn't helped by the fact that, in Ireland, the Church had been going through a tough time of its own. From abuse scandals to clerical misbehaviour and the shocking revelations of the mother and baby homes, the legacy of past controversies had rocked the Church. Mass attendances plummeted, and vocations – once the core strength of the Church in Ireland – dwindled to the point where elderly priests had to continue to serve in parishes long after they should have retired, simply because there were no younger priests to replace them.

Yet faith was something embedded deep within me. If there was one thing I treasured as a legacy of my counselling sessions, it was the critical importance of mindfulness and, in many ways, this emerged as another facet of my personal faith and spirituality.

My upbringing had given me a strong moral compass – and my faith was rooted in doing the right thing, standing up for the truth and trying to live my life according to a set of values. Faith is the opposite of doubt. Unlike my religion, my faith remained an unshakeable belief in something tangible and real based on fact and experience.

For me, how I act towards my fellow human beings is the foundation of my faith. My values are intrinsically linked with honesty, consideration and compassion for others. I believe that doing good for others is, at the end of the day, also good for me. It's as simple as that. My religion shouldn't just be about irregular attendance at church – it should be a daily affirmation of life lived according to a set of values.

When I did go to Mass, I had that inner feeling of reconnecting with a younger self and reaching back to a simpler, happier and more carefree time in my life. When I went to Mass as a child, I never dreamed that such awful, painful events could happen to any family, let alone my own.

It was comforting, in a way, to reconnect with those old feelings of childhood innocence and safety. But I had developed into a more spiritual than religious person. I once heard a great explanation for the difference between the two. It goes like this: a religious person is one who acts out of a fear of the fires of Hell – a spiritual person is one who has been left scarred by those fires through daily life, and yet has learned to live with them and love again.

My spirituality is more my individual practice. It has to do with having a sense of peace and purpose in my life. For me, it includes volunteerism, social responsibility, optimism, contributing to society, connecting with others and self-care.

Healthy spirituality gives a sense of peace, wholeness and balance among the physical, emotional, social and spiritual aspects of our lives. However, for most people, the path to such spirituality passes through struggles and suffering, and often includes experiences that are frightening and painful. I know because I've gone through them in my own life.

Today, one of the most important parts of my spirituality is mindfulness.

So what is mindfulness? In the words of one good friend, it is a brief, daily 'check-up from the neck-up'. It is being absolutely fixed in the current moment. I recently spoke to a friend who does sea swimming twice a day! She said that, for her, it is the most powerful act of mindfulness. The only thing you can focus on is the waves rushing at you, the salt spray, your body's every nerve ending and feeling so connected to your environment. Nothing else exists at that moment.

For me, mindfulness is a few minutes taken each day to run through a checklist of my life. How am I feeling? What is bothering me? What problems do I have and how do I prioritise them? What good things are happening in my life today? What do I have to be grateful for? It is being in front of the fire in your sitting room late on a winter evening and centring yourself to be calm and appreciative of the moment – and being kind to yourself.

For me, it became a daily routine to connect with the day. It might only take 10 minutes, but it would be the best 10 minutes of my day. Sometimes, I'd go for a walk, sit on a bench and contemplate the world around me: the invigorating feeling of an icy wind on your face on a winter day, the breeze in the trees, the song of the birds or even the determined buzzing of a bumblebee on a nearby flower. I would become aware of my surroundings and my place within the world at that precise moment.

I came to understand the critical importance of living in the present – not allowing my day to be dominated by issues in the past, which I was powerless to influence. My strength was in the present, in the 'now' – and I had to keep it focused there.

In the beginning, when I took time out for mindfulness I struggled not to re-run the various traumas of the past – Mags's fatal asthma attack, Jason's brutal murder and Norah's tragic death. After 10 minutes I was more upset, tense and angry than when I had started. It took time to understand how to pause the tape and stop replaying a past I couldn't influence or change. This was a key element of my recovery.

It took a little practice to focus on the present and not drift into the past or future. For me, nature was the key to staying rooted in the 'now'. By taking note of the wonderful things in my life and surrounding me, I drew strength from the day. Nature was an inspiration. The warmth of the sun on my face, the wind in my hair or the cold drops of rain on my skin. Becoming aware of life around me, I came to appreciate being alive in that very moment.

I didn't judge the experiences of my day – I was simply grateful for them, for the simple things of life taking place around me. In a sense, I rediscovered the fact that I was surrounded by life.

When I was in pain, I had nothing to feel grateful for. But when I took the time to clearly consider my life, I had a lot to be grateful for. Yes, I had suffered terrible losses. Yes, the pain from those losses was raw and at times overwhelming. But I had a wonderful husband, four great children, a happy home, a great family and I had my health. So my glass was, when I thought about it, far more than half full. There was also a sense of hope from the fact that the glass was also refillable – and that was entirely up to me.

After Mags's death, I had drifted into a dark place because I cut myself off from all the positives in my daily life. Following Jason's death, I had to be careful not to allow the same thing to happen. My recovery from despair after Mags's death was rooted in embracing mindfulness, and it was something I now practised each day. If it hadn't been for mindfulness I don't know how I would have endured the awful events after 2015.

What I found is that taking a few moments to embrace mindfulness became an escape valve for the stress and tension of my day. On good days, I'd take a few minutes in the morning or lunchtime to walk or sit quietly and take note of the world around me – and then do the same in the evening, sometimes with Sarah. She had grown curious about my commitment to finding quiet times in nature, and asked if she could accompany me. It wasn't long before she began to look forward to our mindfulness sessions, and they became a fixture of our evening routine.

I bought books and audio tapes to help fine-tune my approach to mindfulness. Sitting on a bench in County Clare, staring out at the wild Atlantic waves crashing onto the rocky shoreline and quietly contemplating life became almost like a power bank – I recharged my batteries without even realising they had become drained. Without knowing how, I somehow connected with nature and the universe.

Other times, it could be sitting by a bench and watching the River Shannon flow past Limerick on its way to the great Atlantic Ocean. Over time, I became aware of the changes in the seasons and of the cycles of life. In the beginning, I considered mindfulness and my faith or spirituality to be totally different things. Now, I'm not so sure. I believe my commitment to mindfulness helped me heal – and eventually led me to a point where I was able to re-evaluate my faith.

That re-evaluation was, believe it or not, also boosted by one of the admonitions that Jesus had left us. He advised his followers to be like little children – and once reprimanded adults for trying to prevent youngsters from getting near him. I'd probably heard the story a thousand times or more during the Homily at Masses, and either never bothered to listen or simply didn't understand what it was referring to.

Yet in my own life, there were times when my children taught me more about spirituality and simple faith than I could ever have taught them. I was now at a point in my life where I was well enough to pay attention and learn the lessons on offer.

Jack's and Sarah's talents for singing, dancing and acting had by now become apparent. In August 2019 I travelled to the UK with Sarah to attend an audition for *The Voice UK* that she had been invited to. While in the UK, we went for a walk and happened to come across a church. It was a beautiful medieval church – the kind you see on postcards of quaint English villages. To this day, I don't even know if it was Catholic or Church of England.

On the spur of the moment, I said we would walk in to have a look inside. Without thinking, I suggested to Sarah that we might also say a prayer. I'll never forget how peaceful the interior of the church felt. There was a feeling of safety and calm inside that seemed both welcoming and familiar.

Sarah said she would like to light a candle, and I agreed. Staring around the interior of the church, I didn't pay any attention to what Sarah was doing beyond hearing her rooting around in her purse for a few coins to make an offering for the candle.

When my gaze eventually dropped from the vaulted church ceiling, I realised Sarah was in the process of lighting candles for every person she loved or had lost. In shock, I counted eight candles. Sarah knelt by the candles and began to pray with genuine conviction and focus. When I knelt beside her to offer my own prayers, I felt a strange sort of reconnection.

Having returned to Ireland, I went back to my own church, and this time things felt different. The anger I felt over what my family had gone through had subsided, and I found a sense of comfort from the prayers. In a way, going to church became a form of mindfulness for me – a way to draw strength and healing from the quiet, peace and focus on offer inside.

My commitment to mindfulness is really a no-brainer. I make time for it each day because it makes me feel better. When I take a few minutes daily to connect with nature and the world around me, I am less stressed, more relaxed and have greater enthusiasm for life.

The best way I can explain it is like this. We all depend so much on mobile phones in our busy modern lives. So every evening, we take time to plug the mobile phone in and charge it for the day ahead. For me, mindfulness was the same process for my brain and spirit. But with vastly greater benefits. I am renewed, not depleted.

Thousands of research papers have been published across the world on the benefits of mindfulness and meditation. Experts believe that it is not just good for relaxation and stress-management but can also have an impact on our overall health. Research is now underway into the benefits offered for the treatment of immune disorders and certain chronic health conditions.

Of all the things I tried, nothing helped me as much as my mindfulness 'time outs'. In the quiet, I came to realise that I was powerless to change what had happened or bring those who I had lost back. Slowly, I also came to realise that, if I was to move forward with my life, I had to somehow flick a mental switch between negative emotions over what I had lost and adopt more positive, acceptive feelings of what I still had in my life.

It's not rocket science – if I'm consumed by feelings of anger, pain and fear over the past, how can I hope to move forward to enjoy a present and future filled with love, happiness, contentment and fulfilment? I was essentially throwing away my present because of anger at a past stolen from me. The only person losing out was me.

I began to use mindfulness as a way of accepting what had happened – and as a way to focus on the golden memories of the person no longer in my life rather than the fact that they were gone. In a way, I owed it to them as much as to myself to make the most of my life.

Mindful breathing was a key part of my daily exercise. I'd find a quiet spot, preferably in a beautiful location, and then try to quiet my mind. I'd initially concentrate on making myself comfortable and becoming aware of my place in the current environment. What was going on around me – the feeling of my body connected to the earth, the breeze or sunshine on my skin, the sound of the ocean waves, the birds singing, the insects buzzing around me or the wind in the leaves overhead.

Then I'd focus on my breathing. Usually, I'd have to slow it down, to concentrate on every single breath. Sometimes it took a while to settle into the moment – a steady rhythm of breathing and a sense of calm sweeping over me. If my thoughts drifted, that was OK, I'd just bring them back to the feelings of the moment.

When I'd feel calm and focused, I'd allow myself to think about the loss that was bothering me. Initially, it was overwhelming – the feelings coming in a tsunami. The pain was raw, the emotions white-hot, and feelings like anger and fear bubbled to the surface.

But I'd focus on my breathing and try to picture a single element of the loss. At times it was painful, at times I struggled to control my breathing and fought to simply not break down. Yet the more I practised, the more I got to experience the loss. I felt my grief at a deep, emotional level. Instead of hiding from it, I faced it. The more I worked on it, the less white-hot the pain seemed to be.

As I said at the beginning of this book, I am not an expert. All I know is that practising mindfulness has helped transform my life and given me a peace that, considering all that has happened in my life over recent years, is nothing short of a miracle.

I also discovered that it is alright to feel down. Just as happiness in our lives is normal, so is sadness or 'the blues'. But what is critically important is how we react to it. We all have bumps in the road with our mental health. Every human being who has ever walked this earth has needed support at one time or another in their life.

Understanding this brings its own empowerment. One of the most destructive aspects of my grief was that I somehow felt I had failed. But I came to the remarkable realisation that, by admitting I had a problem and then asking for help, I actually had triumphed.

Across all living things, the solitary being is the most vulnerable. But the living thing that has the support of its family, tribe or, in the animal world, their pack or herd, is immeasurably strengthened.

I realised that my mental health inevitably dipped with the loss of a loved one. Was I overly sensitive to death, loss and sadness because of my lost twin? Had I suffered losses that were simply beyond the human capacity to cope with? The truth is I don't know. But what I do know is that I transformed my life by reaching out for help and by helping others. By trying to cope alone I found the shock and pain convinced me there wasn't any hope of me rediscovering a normal life. Life had been so fundamentally altered that, I thought, it just could not be fixed.

But when I reached out for help – and then accepted the assistance and support offered – I found learning and coping skills to handle my altered life. Yes, I had a void where my loved one had once been. But the grieving process taught me more about myself. My life had changed but, I discovered, so had I.

I undertook classes that focused on introspection and self-discovery. Over time, I not only learned how to handle the pain and grief, but I discovered how to explore who I really was – my strengths, my weaknesses, my vulnerabilities, my ambitions and my fears.

If you had asked me in September 2005, would I have been able to handle the tragedies of 2006, 2007, 2015, 2016 and 2020, I would have faltered and shaken my head. Deep within, I just didn't think I could be strong enough or brave enough. But I not only eventually coped with those tragedies, I helped to coordinate one of the most effective justice campaigns ever mounted in Ireland for a trial in another jurisdiction – largely with the support of Irish people at home and in the US. What a family of supporters to stand side by side in our hour of need.

After the North Carolina second-degree murder conviction of Molly and Tom Martens in August 2017, people contacted me for advice about their own situations regarding loved ones who had died in tragic circumstances overseas.

Not only that, I helped raise my own two children and the two children of Jason and Mags. Each day, I looked at four bright, talented and love-filled young adults and realised that I am capable of so much more than I had ever dreamed possible. Mothering them is my biggest accomplishment.

There are times when I look at my life and draw a dividing line on 2 August 2015. There was Tracey before that date and the Tracey I had to evolve into after that date. The person I had to become was stronger, more courageous, more resilient, defiant in the face of adversity and inexhaustible when faced with impossible challenges.

If I'm honest, I not only like the new Tracey – I am very proud of the person I had to become. Yet I would swap it all in a heartbeat to have my loved ones back.

Over time, I also came to understand how, when we are stressed or feel threatened by events, we humans crave normality and routine. There is a priceless comfort to be drawn from the mundane. It was inexplicable how, in the midst of all the trauma, pain and headlines of the North Carolina trial, I craved normality – a quiet day at home in Raheen with nothing but the school runs, the shopping and maybe the washing to worry about.

In a way, there is a sense of denial to be found in normality. Everyone around you continues with their own worlds as if nothing is wrong. Yet you are bruised, battered and scarred – deep wounds that you are almost afraid to allow to come to the surface. The normal, the mundane helps you to pretend like they are all a bad dream – as if you will shortly awake from this awful nightmare.

But we cannot hide in the mundane forever. The world continues, and somehow we have to find the art of living again. And a key signpost on that road is that the world remembers us not for what we have done for ourselves but rather for what we have done for others. Our actions and not our words are what define us as people.

I also learned that I cannot deny pain, either for myself or for my children. My whole life as a mother has been devoted to protecting my children – even, at times, at my own expense. But I also wanted to give them the tools and teach them all the lessons I had learned over my childhood and adult life. They needed to accept the reality of their lives and learn to live in this world.

As a parent, it is a hard lesson to learn, that you can't teach your children about life by shielding them from it. You don't protect them from pain by teaching them to hide from it. Pain cannot be denied. Life doesn't work that way.

I learned I had to carefully expose them to life, to pain, to loss and to grief when it arose – all the while supporting them as best I could to cope with it and recover from it. I faced pain and suffering knowing I was surrounded by love. My children learned the same lesson. I couldn't ring-fence them from heartache – but I could ensure they lived every second of their lives knowing they were special, were valued and were loved immeasurably.

My family has endured things no family should ever be asked to. That is why I can say, with certainty, that you are far stronger than the things that hurt you. You just have to convince yourself of this truth.

There will be days when the only thing you can do to cope

with your pain is to cry. Don't despair. I came to believe that there is a sacredness in tears – as if they are drops of pure emotion released straight from the heart. They are a mark not of weakness but of power. They show you care – and a person who cares is vastly more powerful than a person who drifts through life incapable of emotion. Tears speak more eloquently than ten thousand words.

But you also need to remember that, while there is a time for tears, there is also a time to dry your eyes and stare clearly at life and your future. Always remember that when you are struggling, self-care should be your priority. Don't force yourself to undertake tasks you are repelled from doing or don't feel ready for. Recovery, at times, is all about taking baby steps and not being afraid to pause until you are ready for something. You will reach your destination, but may just need a little more time to do so.

But there also comes a time for action. In my case, mindfulness helped my spiritual well-being. The better I felt, the more ready I was for action. Gratitude became a cornerstone of my recovery and, in thanks for what I realised I had, I knew I had to display gratitude towards others. Even towards those who had taught me harsh lessons.

In the weeks after Jason's murder and our return to Limerick from the custody hearing in North Carolina, neighbours called to our Raheen home to leave a plate of homemade cookies. They didn't call in for a lengthy conversation about what had happened, they just said how sorry they were for our experience and that they were there for us if we needed anything.

It was such a simple gesture, but it meant so much to all of us. We all felt so fortunate to have neighbours like that. They probably never imagined their gifts would mean so much to us – but they did. It showed they cared. That alone was a balm to our sorrows.

Others contacted us with practical offers of assistance. Did we need any help with babysitting? Could they do the shopping or the school runs? If we needed the lawn cut or garden work done, just give them a ring.

Simple gestures, but ones which meant so much to us. My local community is a wholesome, loving group of people that let us live peacefully and took us under their wings. If there is a Communion event or a bingo, or if one of the girls has a 40th birthday party, a WhatsApp flies around at the speed of light.

In my own recovery, once I was grateful for what I had, I wanted to display that same gratitude to others. So I took a leaf from the playbook of my friends and neighbours. If I know someone who has suffered a loss, rather than ring them for a heart-to-heart conversation about grief that they are probably not ready for, I try to do something practical to help.

I've made it clear that if someone does want to talk about their loss or grief, I'm ready to listen. But I leave the timing of that entirely up to them. I think my experience of speaking out and sharing our experiences makes it easier for people to talk to me. That's OK, as I'm a good listener. I've been where they are, but I also recognise I don't feel what they feel. Emotions are very individual. In the meantime, I make a simple gesture that shows them I care.

Gratitude should be practised when the time is right. You will feel it only when it is true and real to you. Trust me when I say it will feel good to give back, even if you can't bake and return the favour of lovely food given by neighbours. The gesture can take any form. Pick a bunch of flowers from the garden and add a note just saying 'thank you' or 'thinking of you'. These simple notes brought me to tears of joy at the kindness of others. You will feel better, and so will the person who receives it. It also encourages them to do the same for someone else.

Never forget that the most precious commodity any human being possesses is time, and when time is gone, it's gone for good. There is no better gift than offering your time to others – invite someone for a cup of coffee, a lunch or even a walk if you feel they are lonely or isolated. If it is an elderly person, offer to spend time with them in whatever manner they feel happy and safe to accept, be it a cup of coffee in their home or maybe a spin to a favourite spot they are no longer able to reach alone.

When you need convincing, just look around you. There

is something divine about being surrounded by good people, whether they are family, friends or neighbours. It is both motivating and inspiring. None of us can tell what the future will hold, but when you are surrounded by love, you know you can stand and face it together.

Proof, at least for me, of a life well-lived in terms of faith came from my parents. My mother was far more religious than my father – but he had his own set of core values, and wasn't afraid to act when he felt the truth needed to be defended or a wrong righted. In the days after Jason's murder, our family had to rally to raise money to finance the campaign for justice and to ensure we secured custody of Jack and Sarah.

Before the events of August 2015, Dave and I were what you would most likely have described as financially 'comfortable'. We had worked our asses off for the previous three decades. We were about to downsize our house, move into a small property and then buy a holiday home to rent out in France so that we could both retire at 50. After Jason's murder, Dave and I emptied, sold and liquidated whatever we could – all without hesitation – to prepare for the financial demands in the US. It took us all of five minutes to make that decision, and I have never regretted one minute of it.

Somehow, my parents must have realised the financial challenges we faced given the situation in North Carolina. My dad asked me to call over to see him, and I arrived to discover he had taken out his life savings – the money he had been saving for his own funeral. He handed me an envelope containing €3,640 and told me to use it in the fight for justice. It was every bit of savings he had in the world, and it was one of the most poignant moments for me, realising my dad had such faith in me and such a selfless love for his son and grandchildren in the US.

My dad was not perfect – none of us are – but it was proof, yet again, that faith leads us towards being not so much a good person but a better human being. Inspired by the example of others, I wanted to be the best version of myself I possibly could.

Reflection, mindfulness and spirituality helped me identify what my real problems were, what my assets were and what vulnerabilities I had to be careful of. I learned who I really was and what I was capable of becoming.

The tragedies I had suffered had changed me, there is no denying that. The losses of loved ones left scars on an emotional level, and I bear them. But I recovered, and by a process of counselling, meditation, mindfulness, spirituality and a little fun, I emerged stronger, wiser and more attuned to the miracles in my life. I learned that I could either weep over the emotional scars I bore or apply the lessons they taught me in my daily life.

REMINDER

Looking after our mental well-being on a daily basis is the key to unlocking so much of the good that life can give us. But you must allow time for your mind and spirit.

7

RECOGNISING THE RECOVERY IN OTHERS MEANS WE ARE ALSO HEALING

have a good friend who often talks about the fact that you can never fully appreciate healing or recovery in yourself – but you can see it quite clearly in others. By realising others are getting better, it slowly dawns on you that you are healing, albeit sometimes slowly. When you look more closely, you can be amazed at the progress you have made. You have been granted the priceless gift of perspective.

My grief journey was blessed with a wonderful husband, family and four children – including two children who, while I didn't give birth to them, I love every bit as much as if I had. Jack and Sarah effectively became my barometers in life's healing. I could gauge my recovery in them. They became my compass for cherishing all that is good and inspiring in this world. I feel blessed to have Jack and Sarah in my life but, at the same time, I wish to all the depths of my being that the circumstances of their arrival were different.

The death of their mother after an asthma attack and the brutal murder of their father rendered Jack and Sarah as orphans. But the resilience, strength and courage displayed by these two children is nothing short of inspiring. There isn't a day that goes by where I don't draw strength from what they have achieved.

Few children have had so much thrown at them by life as Jack and Sarah. They were aged just eight and ten when they lost their father, their sole surviving parent. Having been brought from their native Ireland to the US in 2011, they then found themselves at the centre of a custody battle just four years later that must have seemed both bewildering and very frightening for them. They then found themselves moving for the second time in their short lives – this time back to Ireland, away from their newly made US friends and classmates. I am certain that there is a particular type of grief that children suffer when being removed from the life they have known – and it ranks alongside the grief of losing a loved one.

Twice in the space of four years they had lost all their friends and schoolmates. Worse still, having lost their mother, they had then lost their father to a brutal murder committed in a house where they were sleeping upstairs. Now, they were learning that the two people they should have been able to trust – their stepmother Molly and step-grandfather Tom – were responsible for making them orphans, and they were also being used as pawns by their stepmother to get away with murder.

No one could have blamed Jack and Sarah if they had emerged wary from the process – unwilling to trust people, constantly keeping their self-protective barriers raised lest they be deeply wounded again by an adult. It would be perfectly understandable if they slightly withdrew from life because of the bruises they had already endured, and for fear of being hurt again.

But the exact opposite is the case. They have grown into confident, talented, kind-hearted and well-rounded youngsters. They have embraced life – worked hard at their personal development, have given back to their community and are dedicated to exploring the potential of their talents and skills. All our children have also developed a group of friends that are loyal, supportive and share the same goals.

Resilient, loyal, generous and loving, our children are models of the sheer courage of the human spirit in times of adversity. I look at each of them and my faith in life is restored daily.

But it wasn't easy reaching this point – and, for some of you, recovery from your own grief will require the same kind of commitment, hard work and support that Jack, Sarah, Adam and Dean were smart enough to accept and committed enough to work towards taking advantage of.

Back in August 2015, when Jack and Sarah arrived back in Ireland, just weeks after their father's murder, it was heartbreaking to see the grief and confusion etched across their innocent young faces. They had lost almost everything – their parents, the North Carolina house they had called their home for over four years, their US school friends and almost every facet of their American lives.

They were back in a country that, although their place of birth, was dimly remembered in their young lives. In many ways, it was a foreign country to them. What they hadn't lost was their Irish family, as well as the unconditional love and support it offered.

In the beginning, it wasn't easy. I'd kiss the children goodnight in their bedrooms and realise they were crying themselves to sleep, heartbroken at the loss of their father and confused over their new place in life. I wouldn't make it two steps down the stairs and I would find myself weeping as well. I could see in their eyes they wanted an explanation – a reason why all of this had been done to them. Part of my pain was that I didn't have any easy answer to offer them. All I could do was reassure them of our family's love and support. That was our starting point.

The death of a parent is hard enough for a child to deal with. But a death that involved a father being effectively ambushed when asleep in bed and murdered by two people who he should have been able to trust? How do you explain that to an adult, let alone a child? It was a challenging time for us, and all we could do was be totally supportive of the children, respectful of their needs and searingly honest with them in everything we did. We also had to explain how they needed age-appropriate support to help them deal with what had happened.

Dave and I had received childcare qualifications as foster parents in the past, and we both understood that Jack and Sarah needed help – expert professional assistance that was beyond our capabilities. Our job was to offer the children unconditional love, support and care – as well as a happy home that made them feel safe and secure. Dave and I decided there and then that we had to listen to their grief far more than asking questions. We didn't need to talk. We practised active listening and responded to their indicators. There were so many markers of progress during the years of healing.

I understood that only through counselling could the children address the deep-rooted issues that, if left ignored, could scar their development in later years and into adulthood. They had endured two of the biggest traumas that any child could possibly suffer, and they needed help dealing with the issues that arose.

Through my childcare training I learned that studies have shown that some difficulties in later adult life can be traced back to unresolved issues from childhood, most especially circumstances surrounding childhood trauma. You can choose to ignore it, bury it deep within you and try to forget all about it. But it doesn't forget about you – and, when you least expect it, the seismic tremors from that deeply buried tumour of hurt can challenge the very foundations of your hard-built adult life.

We were fortunate to be guided towards skilled counsellors in Limerick who had superb experience in dealing with children who had suffered trauma and the after-effects of grief and loss. Over the years, they painstakingly worked through the issues that Jack and Sarah needed to deal with. Some of these were very difficult. Many involved the events leading up to and surrounding the murder of their father. Some involved the way the children had been treated over the years by Molly, the woman her friends hailed as a so-called 'SuperMom'. What healthy person would tell a child from the age of five that their father killed their mother by suffocating her? And that if they told anyone, that he would do that to them too? The psychological implications of what they had just gone through were immense and simply could not be underestimated.

If any mature, experienced adult had gone through what Jack and Sarah had endured through the loss of two parents in such awful circumstances, I suspect they would not have coped as well as these two incredible children. But it was natural that those losses left the children with fears and anxieties. Should the future be feared? What would happen if they were to lose another loved one? Maybe the best way to protect yourself is to maintain an emotional distance from others? How do you process emotions like hurt, fear and anger?

Children – much more than adults – also need reassurance about their role in the events involved. In the case of Jack and Sarah, they were the innocent victims of an appalling crime perpetrated against the person who loved them most in this world. Yet the fact remained, it was Molly who triggered the events of that evening because of her insatiable desire for control of the children.

Reassuring the children was a vital part of the counselling process, not to mention reinforcing the fact that their father loved them, cared for them and would have done anything to protect them. His refusal to allow Molly to adopt them – which we believe was the trigger for the horrific attack that night, amid her fears that the children would be brought to Ireland and out of her reach – was a core part of Jason protecting them.

It took time – months and years of counselling. Don't underestimate the effort that is required. There were days when the frustrations over what Jack and Sarah were working their way through – and my fury at what those two children had been put through by adults and by life – proved so great I wondered if we could stick with the course. There really are the most insidiously cruel and sick people who abuse children for their own warped motives. Sometimes they do it behind a pretty smile.

But we persevered, in part because I realised we had no other choice. The worst thing we could have done for the children was to quit. That would have sent out entirely the wrong message: that in life, when things get tough, you simply stop trying. So we tried it all – art, sport, music, equine therapy, journaling and new experiences. There was also the fact that we could see the counselling was working and the children were slowly dealing with the issues involved.

I wanted Jack and Sarah to leave the emotional baggage of what had been done to them firmly in their past. I didn't want negative elements of their childhood experiences hindering their progression as young adults. They both had such enormous potential in life, I didn't want any brakes being applied to or limits imposed on their aspirations. They had suffered enough. We were all determined to give them the future of limitless potential they both deserved. Jason and Mags would have insisted on nothing less.

There were days when we just had to give them space. At times, I had a thousand questions I wanted to put to them – but I had to bite my tongue and wait for them to approach me. Jack and Sarah needed to know we loved them and would be there for them. They needed their own time and space. As hard as it was, we didn't ask questions – we waited for the time when they felt sufficiently secure and safe to decide it was appropriate to talk.

We also had to learn to see grief from Jack's and Sarah's points of view. We had to learn to speak their language, as it were, in terms of the immediacy of their fears, anxieties and problems. Adults tend to take an extended view of grief. Jason was gone, and I envisioned his loss over the years and decades to come. But for Jack and Sarah, their adored father was gone right now – and if they needed him right now, he wouldn't be there for comfort, advice, to defend them or to offer a shoulder to cry on.

Our greatest fear was that, having lost both their parents, the children would somehow consider trusting and loving other adults to be too risky a business – something that would inevitably leave them vulnerable to hurt and loss. The manner in which Molly had betrayed them and Jason made things all the worse. They simply did not trust adults.

Slowly, we were becoming 'a blended' family, and that also required time. It wasn't just Jack and Sarah who needed time to recover and heal. Dean and Adam were also grieving in their own way. Jason had spent so much time with Dean that our eldest almost hero-worshipped my brother. Adam was Jason's godchild. They both took Jason's loss particularly hard. Dean also idolised Mags and she loved him as if he was her own son. She always said that her one wish was that when she had children they would turn out to be like Dean.

Jason and Mags took Dean camping on holidays when he was younger and were like surrogate parents for him.

Dean has always been full of hope, love and good values. He has a hunger to learn about the world, and is one of the most stubborn people I have ever met outside myself when he is standing up for something he passionately believes in! He is open and giving and has had friends for life since he was nine years old. In other words, Dean grew up to be very much like Jason.

Dean had arrived in our lives a little unexpectedly, when Dave and I were both quite young – but he has been a blessing for us over the years. He had a head of blonde curls when he was born and, as a child, always seemed to be smiling and laughing. His happy demeanour never changed into adulthood, and he is one of the most positive, warm-hearted and dependable people I have ever encountered.

Life wasn't easy for Dean in our early years, when Dave and I didn't have a lot in the material sense of things. We lived in a rented house, and money was tight for several years. Simply ordering a takeaway in those days was a major expense.

Adding to the challenges we faced was the fact that Dean was diagnosed with asthma at quite a young age. He was an inquisitive, active little boy, but there were times when he was quite seriously ill from his condition. Thankfully, it eased as he reached his teenage years, and our gratitude for that was only underlined by what later happened with Mags.

At times Dean also seemed to have a wisdom beyond his years. When I was advised to distance myself from certain people because of the negative influence they were having on my life, I struggled with feelings of regret, embarrassment and lack of self-confidence. Dean was by then in his mid-20s, and he quietly came up to me one day and played a clip from the Canadian psychologist Jordan Peterson to reassure me that what I was doing was correct, and that everything would be alright.

The one thing Dave and I tried to instil in our children was a sense of independence – that our youngsters were confident enough to grow into strong young adults. None exhibit that more than Dean. With his now-wife Kelly, Dean has been an incredible pillar of support for us over a very trying decade. During the demanding 2017 trial process in North Carolina, Dean and Kelly were incredible in their support of Adam, Jack and Sarah.

Adam is our 'strong silent type', with a brilliant sense of humour. Like me, only those closest to Adam ever truly get to know him. He is reserved and decides for himself who he wants to get close to. Adam had just turned 14 when Jason was killed. One day we were on summer holidays and he was hanging out with new friends as a happy, excited kid when the rug got pulled out from under his life.

Everyone was affected, but the tragedy was particularly cruel for Adam in the sense that it sparked upheaval in our world at a very impressionable time in his life. That fateful day in France we were just about to begin a family board game, and then suddenly I was gone from his young life for five full weeks. It is also fair to say that life was never really the same for him after that, with his parents having to travel to North Carolina for various court matters over his uncle's murder for the next few years.

Adam sat first his Junior Cert and then his Leaving Cert exams against the backdrop of the murder trial. I have no doubt there were days when Adam wanted us for his own reasons, but he never asked because he didn't want to distract us from what was happening in the US. He also consistently put Jack and Sarah before his own needs, and in a way that helped them heal together. We couldn't have done it without him.

There was a constant whirl of news around him about his uncle and godfather. He went to school every day – and never once complained. During the intensive support period for Jack and Sarah he was effectively on the sidelines. Because we had to travel to the US so frequently, we missed various events in his life that otherwise we would have been there for. It was two years later before we realised the precise effect this had on Adam and as a family took steps to address it. Sometimes you can overlook the quietest child, as there are so many demands on your time.

My advice would be to look carefully at your children. We were so busy trying to hold down our jobs, provide therapeutic structures for Jack and Sarah and flying over and back to the US for court dates that we missed what was right there in front of our eyes. The truth was that we weren't there for Adam as much as we should have been.

Loyal and devoted to his family, he never once complained. Adam viewed our actions as in the best interests of his family and raised no objections despite the fact that it was our time with him that was suffering the most. He put everyone else in the family first and suffered himself as a result. He paid the price for our work to see justice served for the crimes of others.

But the truth was that while our actions were understandable in the circumstances of all that had happened in the US, they still weren't necessarily in Adam's best interests. We were trying to square the circle, and it just couldn't be done. In trying to see justice done for Jason in North Carolina, we had used the time that should have belonged to Adam – and it was time that none of us could ever get back.

Having realised just how much Adam missed our time with him, we apologised to him. We acknowledged our mistakes and worked really hard to rebuild his trust and our relationship. There may have been no recovering the time we had lost, but Dave and I made extra-special efforts to ensure our time with Adam never again suffered in the future, and that we would be there for him when he needed it.

The bonus was that Adam received an extra brother and

sister. Jack and Sarah dote on Adam and consider him the big brother in their daily lives. When either are uncertain about something, it is Adam they generally turn to first, and Dave and I as parents couldn't be prouder of the young man he has become.

This was one of those factors that prompted me to re-think my arrangements in 2019, and to give up my job to spend more time with my family, with my parents and especially with Adam. My primary message in this is that it is never too late to correct an error and to make amends.

Adam allowed me to rebuild our relationship. We visited my mam together, we did small things together like shopping, having breakfast out with just the two of us and taking time to chat more in the home. I said I was sorry to him. Not being there for Adam at a key point in his life is my biggest regret of those years.

Dave was always sports-mad, and it is no surprise that Adam is the same. They go to major matches together and Adam adores the time he spends with his dad and, on occasion, his big brother Dean. All the boys spend time going to each other's matches. Whoever is playing, they all go along to support. Sarah and I go too, but not as regularly, because those sidelines can be freezing in winter!

Another key element of the rebuilding process was family dinners. We insisted that phones were put away, the TV was turned off and that everyone contributed to the conversation around the dinner table. I wanted us all to eat together – there was no option of people eating separately (without an exceptionally good reason) or taking food up to their rooms unless they weren't feeling well.

On occasions, dinners also featured my parents, Marilyn and Wayne, and our children's cousins. It reinforced a sense of family and of solidarity within the extended Corbett-Lynch clan. There were times we laughed together and times we cried together. But I like to think that, bit by bit, we healed and grew stronger as a family.

The overwhelming sense was that we had each other's backs in whatever life would throw at us. It helped that, within a short time, we could see the benefits slowly emerging in Jack and Sarah. In fact, we all benefited from the process of healing. Dave, Adam, Dean and I realised how important communication was within our new family group. We began to include everyone in the decision-making process. Jack and Sarah felt they were involved in key family discussions – and blossomed as a result. They felt wanted and involved.

In a way, I also considered our close-knit family as a kind of tribe. We were there for each other, no matter what. Our family knew that life could be hard, that you had to work hard for the things worth having and that loyalty was a code for a family to live by. Jack and Sarah were made to feel a valuable part of our tribe and, I believe, settled into their new lives as a result.

Throughout my life, I have always been willing to seek advice and consider new approaches. If I thought it would benefit my family, I was willing to try it. So when friends stressed the importance of daily positivity, I embraced the concept wholeheartedly. I started sending texts with inspirational or uplifting messages to the children old enough to be allowed phones. Every day, I never hesitated to text them telling them how much I loved them. I've no doubt there were days when the children rolled their eyes to heaven with embarrassment at receiving such messages in front of their friends, but I wanted the positive theme to be supporting them every single day. I told all four of our children that, on bad days, it was sufficient to accept that you are enough – that it is enough just to love yourself.

We also took the view that we would never forget the memories of the grief that we had all suffered. The pain was too great, and the wounds too deep for us ever to be able to consign them to the past. It meant emotional honesty for all of us. If we were feeling down, we were honest about it with others. We talked about our feelings, and we didn't hide from them. As a family unit, we tried to support each other and help boost each other's spirits.

Our one rule was that we never judged. I had battled self-doubt my entire life, so I wanted the family home to be a refuge for us all. You could come home, feel safe and share your problems with your family without fear of being judged or ignored. Within our four walls, we tried to keep it simple and ensure that every act was underpinned by love.

Empathy became another cornerstone of our family unit. On a bad day, each of us tried to look at where the other person was. It was essentially trying to put yourself in the other person's shoes.

'Cognitive empathy' was something that cropped up in Jack and Sarah's counselling sessions, and it basically means being empathetic towards someone by thought rather than by action. Nothing was too trivial or small for a show of family empathy.

Over my life, I'd always considered empathy and sympathy to be pretty much the same thing. From Jack and Sarah, I learned that there are very important differences. It was perhaps best explained to me by Sarah when she said during an interview that she felt sympathy is seeing someone trapped in a deep hole but remaining on higher ground and offering them support and encouragement from above. The sympathetic person may also try to simply put a silver lining on the other person's situation instead of acknowledging the person's pain.

Sarah explained that empathy, in contrast, is feeling for the trapped person and the pain they are in, and then climbing down the hole to sit beside them, making yourself vulnerable to sincerely connect with them. It is a desire to be beside them in their pain. The empathetic person will recognise the person's struggle without in any way, either deliberately or accidentally, trying to minimise it.

I also realised we could make new, happier memories of our own. We could re-energise ourselves in life by undertaking new experiences together as a family. There are so many positive things in life if we only take the time to recognise and avail of them. There is no greater truth than the old saying that life is the journey, not the destination.

There is also no vacuum in human existence. If we leave an empty space in ourselves, it will be filled, sometimes by the very things we are trying to escape from, such as negative feelings and emotions. But if you try to focus on the positive – even if only in small ways – it is like a shot of steroids to your psyche. When you associate with good people, good things start to happen to you.

So we started by planning family trips. West Clare was our favourite childhood getaway and, within a short time, it became a haven for Jack and Sarah too. It helped that Jason had brought the children to Clare, and it offered them a connection on a deeply emotional level to their mother and father. Like us, they began to associate Clare with happiness, laughter and good times.

Dave and I invested in activities for the children, from horse-riding and swimming to rugby and music, not to mention surfing, acting, golf and dancing. They were all encouraged to try activities and decide for themselves what they liked and what they were good at. I felt acting was always a good choice, as it built confidence, and it was something both Dean and Adam had participated in from an early age in school. The purpose was not to become an actor but to build self-esteem and challenge themselves.

One key thing I learned was to discover what you enjoy doing. Chances are that if you enjoy it, you will be good at it. But be warned, because sometimes it doesn't work like that. My family takes the view that there should be no limitations in life. You can be whatever you are prepared to work for. Having talent is one thing. But having the work ethic, determination and courage to deliver on those talents is something entirely different.

Adam had a settled routine of rugby and school, as he was older now. Jack and Sarah were so multi-talented that there were times it proved a bit of a headache simply organising their weekly activity programmes from sport to music and from outings with friends to school trips.

Jack loved sports, which was hardly surprising given the time his father had devoted to his soccer, football and baseball in North Carolina. We got him involved in a juvenile rugby club that Dave used to help coach and, within months of being back in Limerick, Jack was never out of his rugby jersey.

Jason's son is deep and complex. He can be reserved around people he doesn't know, but I think that is inevitable given what he has gone through. But when he opens up to people it is a truly beautiful thing to watch. Jack is also loyal and loving and has a deep-rooted confidence that will stand to him in life.

Jack's burden is large, though it is a burden he perceives – even if to him it is quite real. As adults we are responsible for so much, particularly in the legacy we leave children. Molly Martens inflicted a huge burden on Jack, and that is something I will not and cannot forgive.

Sarah is a fascinating contrast to her big brother. Where Jack is reserved, Sarah is outgoing and bubbly. Sarah is very much in my likeness. She is altruistic, volunteers her time for causes she supports and, once committed to something, is absolutely immoveable.

She is also bright, hard-working and adores fashion and music – the latter being a passionate interest that Jack and Sarah share. Again, I suspect this was a direct DNA link to Jason, who had a decent singing voice and loved music, particularly pop and country. As I write this I am brought back to the memory of a small pub in Pallaskenry, where Jason stood singing the Garth Brooks hit 'The Dance', pint in hand. It is a lovely memory of a great night. Sometimes I recall those memories with a hint of melancholy. But I am instantly cheered when I look at Jack and hear his latest musical effort.

What was also interesting was how differently the two children approached their talent. Jack loved performing, but his real joy was in songwriting and composing. Nothing made him happier than working on lyrics or tweaking a hit song to suit himself. He also experimented with his music forms. Initially starting out with classic ballads and pop anthems, he then focused on rap.

His material was so good he was encouraged to post it on social media platforms. Initially, some of his best offerings had deeply personal attachments. Jack liked to post what he considered his best performances as tributes to his mother and father, often around their birthdays and anniversaries. It was deeply personal, very moving and, I firmly believe, very therapeutic for him.

Jack was so good with his compositions that he was offered a place on *Ireland's Got Talent*. However, when it came down to it we both agreed it was more about making personal healing our priority at the time. So despite his wish to sing and share his talent, he opted out, at least for the time being. It was the right decision. He continues to sing and write songs, with some of his compositions being worked on with a well-known studio DJ. He has such amazing songs that resonate with me and everyone else who hears them. I've no idea if he will pursue singing as a career, but Jack's singing and songwriting have emerged as a well of positivity in our home.

Sarah followed suit. But her forte was in live performance, and she was in her element either acting or singing for an audience. When there was no audience available and everyone in the house was busy with homework or chores, Sarah would perform in front of a mirror. She would often record her performances so that she could critique them later and see what she needed to work on. What started out as a childhood passion quickly developed to the point where it could offer Sarah career options.

Her talent was so obvious that Sarah ended up signing with a talent agency. She was offered an opportunity overseas, but it was agreed the timing wasn't in her best interests. Her voice was so good that she was invited to perform with professional musicians around the midwest and, during the Covid-19 pandemic, when everyone was being encouraged to holiday at home, Sarah proved a hit with her favourite songs at impromptu open-air street performances in Clare. A video was taken of one of Sarah's acoustic performances – accompanied only by musicians with a steel guitar and mandolin – and, posted on social media, it immediately went viral. That song performed that day was Sarah looking to rebuild her own confidence after a year in lockdown, and she decided to do it in her dad's favourite place. It was simply beautiful.

Whereas once I would have gone misty-eyed at the pride Jason and Mags would have derived from their son and daughter, my grief journey has reached a stage where, while sad, I can now smile at the realisation that a very important part of the couple is still with us and bringing us joy every day.

Music wasn't Jack and Sarah's only talent. Their counsellors had encouraged them to write about their feelings, seeing it as a form of therapy and release for the children. It also offered a way of identifying what was truly bothering the youngsters after all they had gone through.

In Jack's case, the counselling sessions had an early and unexpected result. Dave and I had tried our best to shield them from the fallout surrounding the build-up to the 2017 trial of Molly and Tom Martens. We kept them informed with the information we believed they needed and deserved to know. But, at the same time, we didn't want the sensational media coverage surrounding the trial to set back their progress.

Our single goal was to protect the children from all that was happening during the trial. But, at the same time, we couldn't keep them entirely in the dark. Dave and I would be in the US for the trial for five weeks while Jack and Sarah were looked after by our adult son, Dean, and our extended family back in Limerick. Our commitment to transparency, trust and honesty meant we owed them the truth about what was happening.

Jack knew the trial was approaching and, seeing me writing in our Limerick home one day, asked me what I was doing. I paused for a moment, uncertain what to say and not wanting to upset him. But then I remembered the counselling sessions and the great importance placed on honesty and transparency. So I explained that I was working on a victim impact statement for the trial. Jack then wanted to know what such a statement was. I explained as carefully as I could, saying that I needed to have a statement ready for the court in case of a guilty verdict, and one in case of a not guilty verdict or a hung jury.

Jack asked, 'Why can't I write one?' I responded, saying, 'You could write one if you feel you need to express yourself.' He didn't say anything else, but I could tell he was thinking things over to himself. Some time later, he approached me and quietly asked if he could write a victim impact statement of his own. My initial reaction was to gently talk him out of it. My fear was that, in writing such a statement, he might set back the progress he had made by weeks or even months. That was totally aside from the upset such a statement might cause him.

I chatted it over with Dave, and we both decided to talk to Jack's clinical psychologist. I was taken aback by the response. She asked us whether we valued Jack's opinion. We both immediately replied that of course we did. The psychologist then said bluntly, 'Jack has a voice and he wants it to be heard – do you think he deserves to have it listened to?'

There was no question after that but that we would agree to Jack writing out his own victim impact statement. I brought it to North Carolina on the torn pages in an A4 pad I had jotted down my own notes on, scribbles included. It was eventually delivered on his behalf by Davidson County prosecutor Alan Martin, and was so powerful that the experienced district attorney momentarily faltered and had to compose himself while reading it aloud to the hushed courtroom minutes after the guilty verdicts were delivered.

Writing proved enormously helpful for Sarah as well, albeit in a different format. As a child, her father would make up stories to tell her and her brother at bedtime and in the mornings. There would be no question of her going to sleep until Jason had delivered the latest epic adventure involving the wonderful characters he had created for his children.

During counselling, we learned that one of Sarah's most vivid memories of her father was the 'Boogawooga' stories he would create for her each morning. No matter how grumpy she felt, she said, Jason's stories would bring a smile to her face. Sarah started writing out the stories she remembered, using characters to distance herself – and then began to weave and create her own tales around them.

I wrote my 2018 book *My Brother Jason*, in large part, because I wanted to counter the lies and fabrications that Molly and Tom Martens had engaged in to avoid justice. My brother's name had been blackened, and I felt honour-bound to defend it and tell the truth about what was done to him.

In early 2019, Sarah came to Dave and me with a series of stories she had written about the adventures of 'Boogawooga'. She said that, since I had got a book published, could she get 'Boogawooga' published as well?

It was deeply moving reading the stories, because, in part, they were inspired by the loss and heartache that Sarah had suffered in her life. When I asked her about her stories, she said she wanted to try to help other youngsters who had suffered losses like those she and Jack had endured. Dave and I agreed she could release it, if it was self-published. So her brothers decided to help her, and they did every step together to support each other.

In December 2019, Sarah launched her first volume in the illustrated 'Boogawooga' series, *Noodle Loses Dad*, at a packed Limerick bookstore. Family, friends, classmates, youth group officials and members of the media all attended on the night. Sarah delivered a wonderful speech, which I had to finish after she became slightly overcome with the emotions of seeing so many people there to show their support to her. She said afterwards it made her feel so privileged that it could help others like her.

The book was later featured on RTÉ's *Late Late Toy Show* at Christmas, and Sarah did multiple readings from her book at children's groups across Ireland for the next few months. The book was even adopted by some youth groups as one of the tools used in helping children to process grief. Orders for the book flooded in from across Ireland, the UK, Europe and even the United States.

Truth be told, the success of the book was very much a secondary priority for me though, needless to say, I was delighted for Sarah that it garnered such a positive reaction. Rather, my focus was on how the book proved Sarah had embraced healing, recovery, the potential of life and her talents. If Sarah could produce a book like this aged just 13, what other incredible achievements might the future hold for her? Here was proof, if it were needed, that the children had used counselling as a bridge to a brighter, better future.

My other personal satisfaction was taken from the fact that, on the rear cover of *Noodle Loses Dad*, there is a verse and a small illustration. The verse reads: 'Angels in Heaven, I want you to know, I feel you watch over me, everywhere I go. I wish you were here with me, but that is not to be. You left me a gift of treasured memories just for you and me.'

The small illustration, in orange and blue, is of two butterflies resting side by side. One is named Mags and the other Ja – poignant references to Mags and Jason. Every time I pick up a copy of Sarah's book, I turn it over to the rear cover, read the verse and then study the illustration – and I smile as I recall Mags's sister, Catherine, describing the sight of two butterflies fluttering over their grave just moments after Jason was buried in August 2015.

If you take the time to pause and consider life, you can sometimes catch glimpses of its cycles and rhythms. Our oldest son Dean married his long-term girlfriend Kelly in August 2021, and their wedding was like a reminder of those golden, innocent days before heartache seemed to camp outside our front door. Despite all the restrictions surrounding the Covid-19 pandemic and the unavoidable reduction in numbers attending family celebrations, it proved an incredible day as two wonderful young people, so clearly in love, walked down the aisle and exchanged their vows.

It was such a special day and, I have to admit, a ray of badly needed sunshine for us all after the toll Covid-19 had taken on our family and the repeated blows we had suffered from judicial developments in the US. The human spirit can take a lot of punishment, but it needs relief and reviving. The wedding was a reminder of the wonderful family memories we had all enjoyed – and would, despite everything, continue to enjoy in the future.

Adam, Jack and Sarah were all involved in the wedding party as groomsmen and bridesmaid. My heart filled with joy and pride that day. It reminded me that, despite my pessimism in my darkest days, life changes and there is and will continue to be good moments. Each person seemed to glow in the photographs that were taken. I was so touched by the magic of the moment that I posted some photos on social media with the message: 'Come live in my heart and pay no rent.'

Life is full of positivity, hope and healing – but you have to be willing to embrace it. For me, happiness is learning to let go of what I thought my life was supposed to be. Instead, I let go and embrace where I now find myself and just how special each moment in life is. I quit trying to make sense of the incomprehensible.

In trying to retrieve my life force, I recovered my soul.

REMINDER

There are times when to achieve happiness in our own lives we should try to help to bring a little happiness to others. Perspective is critical in life, and helping others reminds us to put our own problems in context.

8

ALONE WE ARE VULNERABLE — UNITED WE ARE UNSTOPPABLE

once read that Jackie Kennedy Onassis, the wife of the assassinated US President John F. Kennedy, told friends that no one quite handled death like the Irish. The remark was apparently passed in a discussion about the awful aftermath of her husband's assassination and the elaborate funeral ceremonies in both Boston and Washington.

The funeral became one of the most emotional TV events of the twentieth century, with the striking image of President Kennedy's young son, John Jr, who was only three years old, saluting the flag-draped coffin as the funeral cortège passed on its way to Arlington Cemetery.

Intrigued, I did a bit of reading, not least because I had endured my own share of grief at this stage, and wondered what precisely Jackie meant. Did she think that Irish people somehow had a deeper connection with grief? A greater understanding of how important the ceremonies surrounding the loss of a loved one were for families? Perhaps a reason why such ceremonies had become so elaborate and so traditional?

After all, the current tradition of Halloween traces its roots all the way back to the ancient Celtic festival of the dead, Samhain, where in Ireland the spirits were believed to walk the earth for that day. On Samhain, ancestors became more critically important than ever. The Irish, it seemed, always believed there was a link between the living and past generations – that death was part of the cycle of human existence.

Jackie's connections to Ireland ran deeper than simply being married to the first Irish-American President. She had holidayed in Ireland in 1950 when she arrived in Dublin with her step-brother, Hugh Auchincloss III. There to meet the young Americans was an elderly Irish priest. Fr Joseph Leonard was 73 years old and effectively retired. He had been a close friend of Jackie's step-uncle, W.S. Lewis, for over 30 years, and had offered to show the Americans around Ireland. At this point, Jackie was just 21 years old.

Fr Leonard met them at Dublin Airport and showed them around Ireland, including the major sights in Dublin as well as the Rock of Cashel in Tipperary and the Blarney Stone in Cork. It commenced an unlikely friendship between the elderly Irish cleric and the American socialite who would shortly become the most famous woman on the planet.

For 14 years, Jackie kept in contact with Fr Leonard and, in the weeks after her husband's assassination, she wrote to the priest to confide how she was feeling about his death and the loss she had suffered. 'I am so bitter against God. I think God must have taken Jack to show the world how lost we would be without him – but that is a strange way of thinking to me. I have to think there is a God – or I have no hope of finding Jack again,' she wrote.

When I read those lines I realised that if you substituted the name 'Jack' with 'Jason', it was very similar to how I felt in the days, weeks and months after August 2015. I'm sure it's how many feel when they are grief-stricken. I was bitter because I struggled to understand how such an evil act could be perpetrated against such a kind, generous and good man as my brother by people who thought there wouldn't be repercussions.

The magnitude of what I had read was amplified by all the losses I had suffered. The child within me cried out that it just wasn't fair. Mags dying aged just 31 – Jason's death leaving his children orphaned, the circumstances of Norah Lynch's death, not to mention how swift Kevin's passing was.

Jackie's comments about the Irish having a better understanding of death than most were, I now believe, clearly rooted in the elaborate ritual that has evolved around funerals here. It slowly dawned on me that such funeral rituals were designed to help families – to make the process of saying goodbye that bit easier and to offer people a structure within which they could mourn.

This structure evolved over centuries, with each community having their own traditions to help ease the pain and remind the family how valued their loved one was. In the midlands, there was an old tradition of taking photographs of the deceased as keepsakes. In Kerry, neighbours take turns in shouldering a coffin to a burial plot – and then each person places a single shovel of earth on the coffin once it is laid in the grave. In Cork, if a person is removed or waked from their own home, the coffin is never left unattended – family, friends and neighbours take turns over 36 hours to sit and pray by the coffin.

The old tradition of 'the Irish wake' was designed, I believe, to help families appreciate the beloved aspects of their lost loved ones. Removals were a means of showing how much a person meant to an entire community, or in what great esteem a family was held by their neighbours. Guards of honour were another way of thanking a deceased person for their contribution to a GAA or soccer club, a farming group, a political party or a cultural organisation. Families can be heartbroken and devastated by the loss of a loved one, but it clearly helps for them to realise just how valued and respected that person was during their lifetime thanks to a public tribute.

Psychologists have now argued in favour of allowing

mothers who miscarry babies close to term to be allowed time to hold their dead infants and have time to say a proper goodbye. They are allowed the time and space to grieve. Years ago, the dead baby was whisked away from the parents – almost as if to suggest that by not seeing the dead child it would somehow spare them from heartache. Imagine the pain and silence of knowing there was no chance to hold that little baby. It brings to mind the Irish phrase, 'Tá brón orm', which translates literally as 'Sadness is on me'. You won't be sad or grieve for ever because sadness is not in you, it's on you, but perhaps happiness or contentment can be on you again. At least, that's what I hope for those, including many of my friends and family, who have lost babies over the years.

Back in August 2015, we were shattered by Jason's killing but, at the same time, taken aback by the overwhelming show of support offered to our family by the Limerick and wider Irish community. I was never prouder to be Irish than in those dark days. The solidarity we were shown was incredible. But it is also important to note that the Irish don't have any monopoly on decency – we had astonishing kindness shown to us by American, English, Canadian, Scottish and Mexican people who knew Jason and wanted to show they cared. You hold on to those memories as a positive reminder of the inherent goodness of people.

One thing I held on to from those grim days was how, at our lowest ebb, we were helped by so many voluntary groups – all of whom reached out to us rather than us seeking their aid. Foremost among these was the Kevin Bell Repatriation Trust, which I mentioned earlier, and the community across Limerick.

Colin and Eithne Bell lost their son Kevin in the most terrible of circumstances – the young man was knocked down by a speeding car in Queens in New York as he crossed the road in 2013. The driver never stopped, and vanished into the night, leaving the young man dying by the roadside from catastrophic injuries.

Kevin was only 26 years old, and his death devastated his family. But that brave couple took every parent's worst nightmare and turned it into a mission for good to help others. The fund set up in their son's name has devoted itself to helping families hit by tragedy to get their loved ones home. They turned an awful tragedy into a force for good. Our family, for one, will never forget what they did for us.

On average, the KBRT now helps more than 100 families each year with the repatriation of loved one's remains. They are supported by fundraising from families they have helped, and by those who realise the importance of the work they do. KBRT receives no government funding.

Colin explained that you can't appreciate the impact of losing a loved one abroad until it happens to your own family. 'You probably wouldn't have noticed the number of Irish people dying abroad, but once it comes to your own door, you notice,' he said.

'We help take quite a few people home from England. It is generally €1,200/£1,000 to €2,400/£2,000. From Europe, it could be €4,000 to €6,000. In Thailand, you're up to €7,000 to €8,000. If you go to Australia, it is around €8,000. America is quite expensive, it's generally between €8,000 and €10,000.

'We have a network now of experience and if a family contacts us we can say look you don't have to do another thing we'll look after everything and we'll pay for it as well. The fact we don't need funding from the government says so much for the Irish community. Even today there are three or four fundraisers going on in Ireland somewhere for us.

'It is nearly self-generating the difference for families – [they are] not compelled to do it but most families feel that they are honour-bound to do some kind of fundraiser to keep their loved one's memory alive.'

It all started from an act of community solidarity. As the Bell family were reeling from the death of Kevin and the logistical and financial nightmare of getting his body home to Down, the community stepped in to help. Fundraising across the Newry community raised a total of €180,000/ £150,000.

'I suppose that was the start of it. A couple of weeks after Kevin's funeral we heard about a young fella from Carryduff in Belfast who had been killed in Thailand. So we contacted the parents and said we have this money – we will pay to bring your son home. We kept reaching out, and then we said, look, we will make this Kevin's legacy.'

It is a legacy of kindness and generosity drawn from almost unbearable grief. The lesson I drew from it was to get involved in events to help others. I put my own heartbreak aside and got involved in things to help the community, the vulnerable and good causes. These included sponsored walks, baking challenges, donations, sports events and Christmas carol services.

I had to be ready and capable of undertaking them, but when I did, I not only got the benefit of forgetting about my own troubles for a while but came away lighter of heart because I had done something to help someone else.

Often, we come across someone who helps put our own problems into context. My family has been hit by a succession of tragedies. But we have managed to face them as a united, loving and supportive family. Some people don't have that support when they are trying to cope with grief and loss.

Over the years I have become convinced that every good deed we perform resonates in the universe. It is a lesson worth thinking about. Trust me when I say that for every voluntary event I got involved in to help others, I got more out of it in terms of spiritual recovery and a 'feel good factor' than I ever managed to put in. In some ways I was fortunate. My work with several employers put me in the perfect position to get myself involved in the type of voluntary activity in the community I now wanted to support.

With one health organisation I worked with there were always events in the pipeline – most especially because mental health services in Ireland are chronically underfunded and need every single euro they can get. There's a reason why psychiatric divisions within the greater health service are nicknamed 'the Cinderella' services.

I organised a special boat trip on the Shannon with one brilliant sailing social enterprise called 'Sailing Into Wellness'; I got involved in a Clare beach walk for World Mental Health Day; and, after Sarah published her book, I helped organise the free distribution of copies to charities and juvenile services that worked with vulnerable children. I may have been tired after each event, but I came away feeling re-energised and renewed.

The truth is that there is plenty of inspiration in life if you only take the time to look for it. Limerick is blessed to have J.P. and Noreen McManus and their daughter, who have consistently and quietly used their wealth to help their own community, from generous support of social disadvantage projects to backing of sports organisations working with local youth.

Limerick entrepreneurs Patrick and John Collison have also adopted a similar approach. The Castletroy brothers, who founded the online payments firm Stripe, have taken their philanthropy very seriously both in Ireland and the US. They have been staunch supporters of the American Civil Liberties Union (ACLU), a non-governmental organisation that works to defend and preserve the individual rights and liberties guaranteed by the Constitution and the laws of the United States.

Sadly, the headlines are usually made by the people who follow the lower, more venal road. But there are so many people we can draw strength and inspiration from in life if we only take the trouble to look.

By 2018 I was taking back control of my life. I stuck with my counselling, I was rigorously practising mindfulness and meditation, and the events of 2017 had drawn our family together like never before. But the demands of the US trial and its aftermath had taken their toll. I got the flu and felt very sick. My recovery was quite protracted, and then I got another cold. When I later fell ill with a third bout of the flu I found myself being sent to University Hospital Limerick.

They ran a battery of tests and diagnosed me with an endocrine issue. Dave was convinced my health issues were down to the fact that I was exhausted from the toll of working with the North Carolina prosecutors to prepare for the murder trial, and then the aftermath of the trial itself. Unrelenting stress was taking its toll.

My parents were worried about me, and expressed their concerns. Privately, I was concerned about my health and realised that maybe I was exhausted. But I was even more worried about the consequences of my stepping back from things. What would happen in North Carolina if I took a break and didn't monitor developments with the Martens' appeals?

Gently, my family reminded me that I was no good to anyone – especially myself – if I allowed myself to get so run down that I was ill from exhaustion. I had to re-assert the balance in my life. Once again I was trying to put my arms around the world, trying to deliver the impossible. I needed to relearn that saying 'no' was an important part of recovery.

I had also committed the error of engaging with people on social media who were best left ignored. The people we mingle with in the digital world can have a serious impact on your health and happiness. I understood this, and was very grateful for the way my cousin Nuala acted as a type of gatekeeper for our family in terms of social media in respect of the 'Justice for Jason' campaign. She protected us from so much vile material that some sick people only post in the hope that it wounds or causes offence. If you react to such vile hatred, you've already lost.

Yet I couldn't ignore social media entirely, because using some platforms for engagement was an essential part of my work. I like to keep my interactions online very positive – most of what I post is designed to be uplifting, inspirational and family-positive. For the most part, people respond in kind, and I've made great friends online who share similar goals, core values and commitments.

Not everyone was so inclined. I got drawn into a few discussions that left me feeling guilty, annoyed and occasionally angry. I discovered that some people simply want to unburden themselves of all their negativity – they essentially dump it on someone else. Others just want to start an argument.

Over my life, I could never understand people who take pleasure from fights and confrontation. Some on social media seem to thrive on toxic exchanges. The more bitter, vicious and personal a social media exchange is, the better they like it. Some posts are simply about baiting others. Invariably, those people are also posting behind the safety of anonymity – hiding their identity behind a social media 'tag' or 'handle'. I ultimately feel sorry for such people, because I believe only someone living in an awful position in their own life could draw any pleasure from such toxicity. If you only deal in poison, you'll end up being poisoned yourself. It is a dangerous currency.

So one of the first things I did was to undertake an online spring-clean. I removed anyone from my social media interactions who made me feel guilty about the blessings in my life. I said 'goodbye' to everyone who I considered dealt in only negative emotions. My priority was to avoid drama in my own life so why on earth was I engaging in such drama online? Even if I wasn't posting material about such rows or online disputes, I was mentally drawing from it.

It dawned on me that once again I had acted out of fear. I was afraid to block people who were negative because I was worried about what they might think or say about me. Then I realised that they probably didn't even realise I had distanced myself from their negativity. I felt so much better when I blocked them, and they likely didn't even know I had vanished from their feud-filled world.

The online world can be a wonderfully supportive place. It can offer information, contacts and new directions to our lives. But it can also be a minefield to the unwary or innocent. If we are feeling low or vulnerable, even the most innocuous online comments can hurt. Sadly, some parts of social media platforms are little more than a sewer, and I owed it to myself to steer well clear.

Lots of people offered advice. Almost all of it was well-intentioned. But some things that people said I found hurtful. When it comes to issues of grief and loss, it is better to say nothing than to offer advice that could cause hurt or offence, even if it is unintentional.

It was around this time that I came to believe that the seven stages of grief were largely bullshit. There may well be seven stages of grief, but they are not linear, and often are not chronological. From my bitter experience, they can occur and reoccur totally out of order.

With grief, we are working towards acceptance – a realisation that the life we once enjoyed with our loved one is over and will never reappear. We come to understand that we have a new life to lead, one where they are with us in memory and in our hearts, and we are grateful for them having been in our lives.

But just because I have accepted the loss today doesn't mean I won't struggle with acceptance tomorrow or on the date of a significant anniversary. It is a constant, evolving and cyclical process where we need to stack the deck in our favour with positive behaviour, good associations and coping mechanisms for when things go wrong. Because, as we all know, they will go wrong!

There are times when the darkness around us makes the light of hope seem all the brighter. Each one of us needs joy and happiness in our life. They are the reminders of all that is good in life, and markers on our journey back from grief.

I took that concept and applied it to the dark events in my own life. Over the years I had come to dread all the anniversaries associated with the people I loved and lost. Their birthdays, their wedding anniversaries and the dates of their death. It all served to remind me that they were gone and highlight the voids in my life.

When I was ready, I decided to change the process and, instead of reminding me of their loss, those dates would now remind me of their lives, their goodness and their legacy.

Most of all, it reminded me how they had lived and *that* they had lived – and that I had been blessed to share in part of the journey. It wasn't a case that I believed they were somewhere better or somehow better off. The light of hope would start to banish the darkness that had enveloped us.

I started with my brother Jason. Ever since his murder, I dreaded all the anniversaries of his life, because they threatened to bring back all the pain, suffering and grief in a tidal wave of emotion. Now, I wanted to celebrate the fact that I was lucky enough to have had such a brother, even if it was for just 39 years.

Starting with what would have been Jason's 40th birthday, we transformed an event of negative emotions into a celebration of his life. We all gathered at Spanish Point in Clare – a place of golden childhood memories for all the Corbett family – for a special day. We had a wonderful meal, we told stories about Jason and then we went to the beach, where we lit a bonfire, scribbled messages of remembrance and attached them to Chinese lanterns, which were released into the skies over the Atlantic Ocean and the rugged Clare coastline.

Life isn't an existence. It was designed to be lived – to extract the full value from it you have to risk the lows in life as well as the highs. A friend once offered me great advice as regards the options we have when faced with fear – we can either 'face everything and recover' or 'fuck everything and run.' I decided to go with option number one.

I decided it was time to stand my ground in life, make sure my candle of hope was burning brightly and savour every good thing that I was blessed with. Yes, I had suffered terrible losses. Yes, I missed the loved ones who had passed. Yes, there were days when I felt vulnerable, hurt and afraid, times when the darkness of loss seemed inescapable.

But I was also surrounded by a wonderful family, buoyed daily on a tide of love and support, and had the opportunity to develop my potential in any way I chose. My recovery was all about perspective – should I live my life based on what I had lost or what I still had? Do I ignore the remarkable blessings that surround me each day because I miss one from my past?

In life, I had to stop worrying about the unknown. It was time to refocus on trusting that good things will happen and being ready to appreciate them. My priority had to be on becoming the best possible version of myself. The young Tracey loved adventures and trying new things. Whether it was a new restaurant, a new lifestyle activity, a new country, a skill programme, a food I hadn't tasted before – though initially fearful, I revelled in pushing myself outside my comfort zone. With each new experience, I felt I became a more polished version of my true self. I was delivering on the potential that Tracey had to offer.

It was time to rediscover that ebullient version of me that was buried deep inside. I wasn't an economic unit put here to focus on earning a wage, cooking meals and helping pay a mortgage. Reconnecting to the young and ambitious Tracey who was in love with life was a key part of taking my recovery to the next level.

It was my mother who taught me that lesson. She loved life to its fullest degree – and had an instinctive sense of what was really important in life. Best of all, she exuded love and support. People adored being around her because of it. People felt better for having met her. Taking a leaf from her book was one of the smartest things I ever did.

In 2017, I was akin to an empty vessel. I needed to be inspired, to re-educate myself, to challenge myself to rediscover life's meaning, to empower and motivate myself. I needed to relearn how to embrace my life, to be empathetic, and to understand and above all listen to myself and others. There were a number of things I learned when searching for answers.

Ask yourself, when somebody says something you perceive as harsh, unjust or hurtful or just stupid – was that their original intention? In grief, I became so hyper-sensitive that my emotions were all over the place. It was a roller coaster, and not a very exciting one, more like those that leave you nauseous after the ride.

I realised that people would feel awkward meeting me, as they would be confused and uncertain about what to say. Our family had suffered so many losses that they wouldn't know whether to ignore the tragedies or to refer directly to them. In the confusion, they would make remarks that were unhelpful, inadvertently hurtful and unintentionally crass. In some cases, the remarks could even be highly offensive.

Try not to take it too seriously, because not everyone thinks as you do. We are all unique and individual. No two people think the same way. How someone reacts to you can be down to the way you articulate yourself, something happening in their own sphere entirely unrelated to you, or it simply could be that they're having a bad day. Bear in mind that we all have times when our brain becomes disengaged from our mouth.

No one has a monopoly on pain, trauma, grief or anger. I guess that's the thing about the world that I have learned; we really need to have more empathy and be more attuned to each other's need for support. Grief is a bit like an invisible cloak so many of us are carrying around. People see us but they somehow don't recognise the suffering we are trying to cope with. They see the public mask – only a few are shrewd enough to determine the emotion behind the mask.

When I made efforts to get healthy, I looked really good and felt equally as positive. But there are always naysayers and critics. On one occasion, I was going to an important work event. It was my first outing after returning to work from the North Carolina murder trial. I was nervous about all the questions I would have to face when the person who I was with turned to me and said, 'Look at you, you look so nice – and you are making me feel so old and awful.'

They didn't just say it once to me – several times over the course of the evening the same comment was passed to me. Clearly, they weren't intentionally trying to wound me and, clearly, they did not feel very good about themselves. I think they were trying to build me up at their own expense. But here's the thing. Not only did the comment make me feel like crap, I was uncomfortable and stressed about it.

The same person had been angry for a very long time – I knew all about it because they too had lost someone very dear to them and struggled to cope. So I understood that they were stuck in their own angry mire of grief. Some of us can remain trapped in that when something like murder becomes part of your life.

The point I am making is that their intention should be immaterial to me – whether they were trying to be passive-aggressive, complimentary or trying to put me on the defensive. The result of their comment was entirely down to me. I was the one who chose how to react and feel. My well-being was my responsibility. The choice whether to take something as a positive or a negative was entirely down to me. That was my power. The option to take the high road, take a compliment where perhaps one wasn't intended, focus on the positive in an overwhelmingly negative situation was entirely down to Tracey.

A key part of my ongoing recovery was a determination to distance myself from such negativity in the future. I did this for my self-preservation. Always try to surround yourself with positive people. Those who will reinforce your hard-won recovery efforts. Never forget that if you think you know what is going on in someone else's mind, the chances are you don't.

It helps to take people at face value. Over the years I wasted so much energy trying to second-guess situations when I could have saved myself so much mental anguish by just choosing to see and accept a positive outcome.

Today, if somebody said to me, 'Tracey you look so dressed up and I look awful now,' my response would be, 'Thank you, I'm working really hard to be healthy and well in myself. It took a lot of hard work but it's paying off. I'm sorry you feel unhappy. I can share what I did if it helps?'

Be careful not to be overly sensitive during times of grief. All our senses are heightened. If you are worried or concerned and want to know why somebody said a specific thing or what somebody is thinking, then my advice is to simply ask. If they don't want to tell you what's on their mind then that's on them. Your side of the street is now clean.

Sometimes we don't want to disappoint or change people's expectations of us so we avoid hard questions. Understanding that this is a fact of life is important for us. Responsibility for ourselves and for the truth of our own feelings is part of the recovery process: accepting that we are not perfect, we are not always right, we don't have the monopoly on grief and pain, we are not the best human being on the planet – but neither are we the worst. We are simply human and trying to do our best, one day at a time.

At times of doubt, there is nothing more reassuring than positive action, either for ourselves or for others. This was the most important thing for me during all my times of grief. After Mags's death, I took the positive steps of seeking help and changing to a healthier lifestyle. When Jason was murdered, I took action to protect Jack and Sarah. When Norah died, I did my best to help Dave and his family. When Mam had her heart attack, I acted to put her and my dad first, ahead of work concerns.

Be active. Care for yourself and the people in your world, your tribe, your crew and your family. My advice is not to wait another year to make time for that planned break; don't wait for divine intervention or put off a family event because you're too busy with work. If that beautiful dress looks amazing on you – don't put it back in the wardrobe, wear it to dinner. Don't wait to take your kids away and sit by the sea to let the sunshine warm your face as they play in the surf. If you can do it, then get it booked and get it done. The greatest toll grief can exact on us is to waste today and postpone the positives in our life for a tomorrow that never comes.

So, taking my own advice, a few years after Jason died, we returned, a very different family, to France. This time Dave and I travelled with Adam, Jack and Sarah. We went to the same holiday park because it was familiar and felt safe, which was paramount for the children. I have to admit the choice did give us cause for pause. It brought back memories of that awful day in August 2015. But to honour Jason and all those we had loved and lost, we had lives to live.

As it transpired, it was just what we all needed to bond. We had a barbecue each evening. Dave and I kept it simple, didn't try to undertake too many excursions, and we all slowly relaxed and enjoyed each other's company. The children led the way and made friends with youngsters from all over Europe. Seeing the innocent happiness on the children's faces was like a balm for Dave and me. We watched as the children made memories that helped them recover from their own grief. We all need such memories.

Ever since I was a child, Adare Manor in Limerick was like a fairy-tale castle to me. Everything about the architecture and grounds created vivid dreams of the life of a princess in my mind. Adare was just the most magical, safe and picturesque place I could imagine. Dad had once brought us to the abbey across the road. I was very young, but I was captivated by Adare. That feeling never left me.

But I had never been inside Adare Manor. I had no idea other than a glimpse of it from a distance when I was really young and then images from books I read as I grew older. For decades, I was mesmerised by the house and gardens, but somehow felt it was a place for other people and not for me, perhaps a reflection of the self-confidence issues I had in my early adult life.

With Mags, I began to tackle that lack of confidence and explore places that I secretly longed to experience but was somehow afraid to try. Thanks to Mags, we treated both our mothers to champagne on Mother's Day – something none of us ever forgot and I drew enormous joy from. It was such a treat. We sampled good restaurants and travelled to places that I could only have dreamed about as a teen.

When she was gone, I felt for a time like my confidence shield had been taken from me. In recovery from grief, I realised Mags had given me a gift – she had introduced me to the confidence to push my boundaries, to sample worlds I thought were beyond me and to expand my knowledge of the world. I had wasted years being afraid to experience new things. But that would no longer be the case – even if I had to find the courage to seek out these new experiences on my own.

For me, Adare represented a version of me where once upon a time I would have felt that I didn't belong or was somehow out of place. There was always something else to spend our hard-earned money on. But I know better now because it is all relative to me and those I love.

I made lists of things I wanted to do: get healthy again, rebuild myself, find balance in my work by doing something worthwhile while earning an income, visit Sandals resort, retire to be with our children by my 50th birthday, learn to play golf, and accept that it is perfectly alright at times to put myself first. So, I knew a visit to Adare Manor would be on my agenda once the special occasion arose. That arrived with Dave's 50th birthday.

All we ever wanted to give each other as gifts was time together. So now I had the perfect opportunity. I booked Adare and, as I hoped, it was as exceptional a visit for Dave as it was for me. The children joined us for a surprise dinner, but the overnight stay was for Dave and myself. To describe the experience as magical fails to explain what it meant to us all.

We had been battered by grief and tragedy. It is not to stretch the point to say that repeated tragedies had literally brought us to our knees as a family. But we had not only survived but recovered stronger and drawn even closer as a family unit. Now, we would celebrate life together, forge wonderful new memories together and honour those we had been privileged to spend time with.

Please don't think it is about money. We didn't sell everything we owned, mortgage ourselves to the hilt and jet off to Barbados to blow every euro we had. Our budgets stayed the same, and takeaways were still a weekend-only treat. We were careful with what we spent. But we began to invest in ourselves and our loved ones. Time was truly our currency, and we began to spend it wisely. Adare wasn't about spending money – it was about re-joining life and creating new memories.

On 26 December 2018, my husband gave me another perfect fillip after three years of grief and loss – and helped me cross a second major item off my bucket list. I always joked that Dave's first proposal when I was 19 should go down as the worst proposal in history. I remembered that night, and would recall to my friends how he waited until 11.30 p.m. in a rain-filled, bitterly cold night outside and said, 'Well, will we get married?' I had to help him up from his bended knee he was so frozen.

So it was a complete shock when on our first trip away to Venice in years he re-proposed outside the Grand Café in St Mark's Square with the orchestra playing 'Don't Cry For Me Argentina', which I loved! You can imagine the shock – I wouldn't have expected it in a million years.

When we returned, Dave suggested that we renew our marriage vows. The suggestion that we do so seemed a great way to bond our blended family, not to mention being perfectly timed. It also reminded me just how much I loved him – and how fortunate we were to have found each other. I am so genuinely glad I embraced the chance of such a magical day because those moments can be so fleeting.

Our little tribe went out of their way to ensure the day was memorable. The vow renewal ceremony wasn't just the best Christmas present my husband could have offered me

– it was one of the most important gestures of my life. Dave has been my rock, my best friend and my life companion. I considered our marriage vow renewal a form of validation of our almost four decades together.

My sister Marilyn was the celebrant, Adam escorted me to the altar for the ceremony, Jack sang a beautiful song, Dave gave the most moving speech and Sarah performed a special dance. Most magical of all, Dave and I renewed our vows on the very day that was my Mam and Dad's 51st wedding anniversary, something they took tremendous joy from. It was quite simply the perfect day. In a special way, Mags, Kevin, Norah and Jason were with us, because we carried cherished memories of them all in our hearts.

I'd learned to treasure the wonderful moments in our lives, so I had arranged for artist and videographer Luke Culhane to capture the special ceremony for posterity. That most magical day is there for me if I need renewal or inspiration in the years ahead.

A few years back I was at a humanist wedding ceremony. One of the focal points of the ceremony was a special box of memories that the celebrant advised the bride and groom to use for cherished keepsakes of their courtship. Into the box went photographs from a holiday they had enjoyed, an empty bottle of aftershave from the first Christmas present she had given him, a St Valentine's Day card he had sent his beloved and the menu from their wedding luncheon.

The celebrant said that, if troubled times ever arose during their marriage, the box should be opened and used as a reminder of what they had shared together – and of the love they had professed to each other. It should be kept safe and, if possible, they should add items to it over future years to reflect special times spent together.

Whatever about marriage, life is precisely like that. In my experience, we need to constantly update our happy memories. We need to keep a lovingly maintained inventory of all that is positive, good and wonderful in our daily life. Because when the dark days arrive and tragedy strikes – and invariably it will – you have that golden treasure chest of happiness and hope to fall back on.

All of which helped me understand what Jackie Kennedy Onassis had meant. Her view of how the Irish handled death – the intricate web of events surrounding the death of a loved one: the Rosary, the removal, the funeral itself and the traditions around the graveside – was born from her own harrowing experience of loss and her exposure to how an Irish family and community deal with grief.

If you've any doubt about how seriously Irish communities take grief and loss, just go to your nearest cemetery for All Souls Day. Not only will you see graves that have been cleaned and decorated with fresh flowers but you'll also see large numbers of people gathered for the special blessing of all those who have passed away. These ceremonies even take place in cemeteries that are full and long since closed to new burials.

It is a similar story at Christmas. A stroll around your local graveyard will reveal dozens of graves with special Christmas wreaths, candles and mementoes. Loved ones are particularly missed at such traditional family times at Christmas, and grave tokens are a symbol not just of the cherished role someone once played in our lives but a tangible reminder that while they may be gone, they have not been forgotten by those they loved and were in return loved by.

For a long time, I viewed such things as memorial cards and anniversary notices as little more than commercial gimmicks – part and parcel of the industry which has sprung up around death. I understand better today. While they may not be for everyone, they can help with the processing of grief.

When a relative of mine passed, we discovered a lovingly-cared-for collection of memorial cards in her home – it was essentially a treasury of life. She had stored cherished memories of every person she had known, loved and lost – all preserved in a drawer, right beside her prayer book. The cynical might view it as a catalogue of death. But I've learned better. It is more a chronology of life – a reminder of the special people we have shared time with, played alongside as children, laughed with as adults, worked with, sat down for Christmas dinner with and gone on holiday with.

Remembering such people – especially in prayer – is the greatest honour we can pay them. In a way, by remembering and honouring them, we also honour ourselves and the life we have lived.

REMINDER

There is a reason we have such a strong community involvement in funerals and grief – it helps ease our burden of loss and underlines just how much our loved one meant to the community and not just to us. Grief shared is far easier to carry.

9

SETBACKS ARE OK – IT IS HOW WE RESPOND THAT MATTERS

n February 2020, most of my priorities were focused on events in the US. We were by now over a year waiting for the decision of the North Carolina Court of Appeals in the challenge by Molly and Tom Martens to their murder convictions. It was a long and difficult wait. There is no point in denying that it took a toll on our family.

I did my best to stick to my wellness plan, tried to focus on the positive and felt ready to deal with the worst that could happen while praying desperately for the best. But, like millions of others around the world, my priorities were about to be radically altered by a tiny virus called Covid-19.

At first, like everyone in Ireland, we thought this was something that would only affect China and parts of the Far East. We had all been lulled into a sense of complacency by the false alarm over the feared SARS pandemic in 2002/3. At the very worst, or so I thought, this Covid-19 virus might result in some restrictions on long-haul air travel. The scale of our interconnected world was underestimated by almost everyone.

Over the days and weeks, the TV and newspaper headlines came to be dominated by the deteriorating Covid-19 situation globally. The first cases of the virus were detected outside the Far East. Then we watched in growing apprehension as China went into full lockdown, new hospitals were built overnight and confusion over the scale of the death toll mounted.

Our family then suffered a double blow that once again left us reeling. The North Carolina Court of Appeals upheld the challenge taken by Molly and Tom Martens by two votes to one. It was a critical setback, because we had firmly believed that the original trial was entirely fair. But the Martens family had the funds to mount major legal challenges, and they had raised just enough doubt over legal technicalities to persuade two judges to rule against the original conviction.

We knew the North Carolina Attorney General would immediately challenge the ruling to the Supreme Court. It was cold comfort, because it appeared to us that Jason's killers already had one foot out of their jail cells.

Try as I might to look on the bright side – or even to find a bright side – I knew this was a major setback. That was why Dave, Marilyn, Wayne and I had travelled to Raleigh in North Carolina for the Court of Appeal hearing in January

2019. I knew it was important, and that we needed to be visible there. Ultimately, we travelled across the Atlantic for a hearing that lasted literally less than two hours.

We thought that was the worst life could throw at us. How little we knew. Just weeks after the Court of Appeals ruling, the pandemic hit Europe with a ferocity that hadn't been experienced for over a century. First, we thought it would only impact Asia, but then it hit Italy. Spain, France and the UK were next, and finally it struck Ireland.

We watched in horror each night as our TV screens showed hospitals battling to prevent themselves from being overwhelmed by the numbers of people critically ill from the virus. In London, even the army were drafted in to help build a vast new hospital entirely from scratch.

I think everyone in Ireland felt a shiver of fear, because we knew our hospitals had far less surge capacity than these other European countries. Over any average year, there were major queues at Irish acute hospitals because of a chronic lack of bed space and intensive care unit capacity. We all began fervently disinfecting everything.

Almost everything we took for granted in our daily lives was suddenly suspended as the government imposed a strict series of lockdowns aimed at controlling the spread of the virus and buying desperately needed time to protect the health system. I knew from past experience that Ireland's emergency medical capacity was already overstretched – you only had to look at the queues at emergency departments in Limerick, Cork and Dublin each winter to realise the system was creaking under the weight of demand.

Our home was just a few minutes' walk from UHL, and each winter it was one of the worst-hit by waiting lists at the emergency department. There were times over previous winters when the emergency department at UHL resembled a war zone. If a normal winter flu outbreak could do this, what would Covid-19 now inflict?

My immediate fear was for my mother and father. They were both in their 80s, and I didn't need RTÉ or Virgin Media news bulletins to tell me that they were in the most vulnerable category as the virus started to cut a swathe through Irish society. It had also been less than a year since my mother's heart attack, and she was still very frail.

Almost from the outset, the elderly and those with underlying health conditions were in the firing line. Nursing homes, in particular, were the focus of early concerns, as people scrambled to try to protect the vulnerable. The elderly or the sick living at home were urged to 'cocoon' and protect themselves from the virus.

It was like being caught in some kind of strange science fiction story. Everything we took for granted about daily life was suddenly either gone or restricted – visiting family, travelling, eating out, going to a café or pub, heading to the cinema or enjoying a concert.

Our parents depended greatly on us. But, when the government advised elderly people and the vulnerable to cocoon, we knew Mam and Dad had no choice but to go into a protective 'bubble' for their own safety and welfare. We now had to limit callers to my parents' house in a bid to protect them.

We would drop messages and essential supplies at the front door of their home and then wait outside the front wall for them to collect them. None of us went into their home for fear we might accidentally bring the virus with us, unless it was for medically important reasons, such as administering injections. Only vital health care workers would visit their home.

I ensured Mam and Dad took all precautions and had a plentiful supply of masks, gloves and hand sanitiser. But they were both too elderly to entirely look after themselves, and they depended on the support of their weekly home helpers.

The timing couldn't have been worse in terms of my mother's health. The previous summer I had travelled to the US with Sarah to support her dream of forging a career in the entertainment industry. Sarah's voice and performance skills had continued to develop, and people within the Irish entertainment industry advised us she had very special talent.

In August 2019, Sarah had been invited to participate with other talented youngsters at a special workshop in California. It took place in Los Angeles, and was aimed at helping young aspiring singers, dancers and actors to prepare for a career in the industry. Thousands of youngsters from all over the world attended, and the training camp culminated in a special awards ceremony.

Sarah won gold in two categories and silver in the other two. She was simply sensational during her sessions. It was the best thing to have happened to her, and we were all bursting with pride. Because of her success, she was immediately approached by two agents based in Los Angeles. But I felt she was simply too young, Los Angeles was too far away and it was best for Sarah – particularly after all she and Jack had gone through – to stay in Limerick and remain focused on her education. It was still a wonderful boost to Sarah's confidence, and everything about her sparkled as a result, from her eyes to her personality.

To add to the joy of the moment, Dave had flown out with Adam and Jack to join us. The plan was to have a short family holiday on the California coast. It was the tonic we all needed. I was particularly looking forward to seeing Monterey, a place I had fallen in love with, having been captivated by it in the *Big Little Lies* TV series starring Nicole Kidman and Reese Witherspoon.

It was a bit of a wellness reward for me. Some people use the phrase 'grief travelling'. In fact, travel can provide many forms of support during grief. It can be restorative, healing and commemorative. Think of the many people who travel to Lourdes or journey the Camino de Santiago. You can travel to remember a special loved one, and for me that's when we visit Spanish Point in County Clare. It is very helpful to connect memories in order to feel closer to our loved ones by returning to a place of positive memories. It helps to recall the love felt. This felt like a restorative holiday for us all. What better elixir for life than to travel and have new experiences?

It had been five tough years since Jason's death, and this holiday was all about sharing family time and recharging our batteries. Being able to celebrate Sarah's success made it all the sweeter. Our plan was to visit Los Angeles, Lake Tahoe and finally Monterey before heading home. I also wanted to devote plenty of time to Adam.

A few days into the break I realised that I was at my best – my healthiest and most content – since Jason's murder in 2015. For years I felt I had the weight of the world on my shoulders. Now, I felt as if a burden had been lifted from me, and I couldn't wait for each day to begin.

We did everything together as a family – toured the sights, sunbathed, swam in the Pacific and laughed as Adam and Jack tried their Irish charm on the fabled California girls. After a few days, it was easy to understand why so many people want to live their lives in California, as it boasts such a life-friendly environment. I also relished the opportunity to be anonymous. No one knew us or our history, and it gave us all freedom we never realised we had lost. It felt good to position our good health holiday as a lifestyle priority.

It was just into the third week when, once again, a phone call from home changed everything. We had awoken after another glorious day on the beach in Lake Tahoe. Jack had gotten a little sunburned for the first time, and we had spent the evening in one of the hot tubs, relaxing and taking it easy.

We had ordered takeaway pizza, and were planning on moving on to the final stop of our US holiday. Everything was packed, and we were ready to hit the road to Monterey. I was beyond excited, because the following day was also our wedding anniversary. Dave had organised a beautiful hotel overlooking the sea, and a romantic dinner was booked. After years of trauma, I was optimistic and life suddenly felt good again.

I can still picture the children sipping their drinks, munching on cinnamon buns and enjoying the simple pleasures of life – all chatting excitedly about what they were going to do in Monterey. Just as we were about to head towards the highway, my phone rang. Marilyn was calling to say that Mam had fallen ill. The details were sketchy, and our family were still awaiting the results of tests conducted on her. But it was clear from the tone of Marilyn's voice that it was very serious.

All I could gather was that Mam was feared to have suffered two heart attacks, and was now in the intensive care unit of UHL. Dave – just as he had in France in August 2015 – immediately supported whatever decision I wanted to make about going home.

I felt totally panicked and helpless. I was on the other side of the world and, even if I left for the airport now, it would take me 24 hours or more to get to my mother's hospital bedside. Dave parked our rental car in a lay-by and kept the children occupied while I made some urgent phone calls.

With the support of our airline and community advocate, Senator Maria Byrne, I was able to get our return flights changed so we could race back to Limerick. Then I managed to get a call through to the doctor treating my mother for a detailed update on her condition.

I discovered Mam had suffered one heart attack on Saturday and a second two days later. The tests revealed she had a blocked artery. Ordinarily, that would be dealt with by immediate surgery. But the doctors involved decided my mother's age and general health condition ruled out such major surgery. It was simply too risky.

Mam was also on Warfarin as a blood thinner. In the end, doctors decided they would try to treat the condition through medication, and Mam was allowed to return home after recuperating in UHL for several days.

Her doctor said that she needed a comprehensive care plan to be put in place. Without it, her life expectancy and quality of life would be severely reduced. My father was also in poor health, but he was now acting as the main carer for his adored Rita.

After chatting with her doctor, I realised that the damage to my mother's heart was quite severe. Like never before in her life, she now needed her family to rally to her side and her care. Years of recovery and mindfulness had taught me to think with a clarity that allowed me to focus on what was really important at that moment in my life. Right now, looking after my Mam was my overriding concern.

Two days after Marilyn's phone call, we arrived back in Limerick from the US. Arriving at my mam's bedside was very emotional – tears were shed, hugs were exchanged and I quietly made a vow to myself that I would be as good a daughter to my mother as she had been a wonderful mother to me.

I talked it over with Dave and came to the decision that I would leave my job with the non-profit and take over the care of my parents. Ever since I was 16 years old, I have worked, and, thanks to hard work and perseverance, I had risen to a management role with lots of responsibility that I loved.

There was a lot of soul-searching, but I was convinced that what I wanted to do was correct for both me and my family. As always, Dave was 100 per cent behind me. All he wanted to know was that I had carefully thought it all through – if that was my decision, he was supportive. Once again, I couldn't have asked for a better soulmate.

The children were of the same mind. They were also quick-witted enough to realise that, by giving up my job and taking over care of my parents, I would inevitably have a lot more time for them. Dean, Adam, Jack and Sarah adored our family time together and believed my decision would benefit them as well. Sarah put it best when she said, 'Before, you had to make time for us all – now you have the time.'

In hindsight, it was one of the best decisions I have ever made in my life. This was just six months before the pandemic erupted, and none of us had any inkling of how utterly our world would change.

But for those six months I had the blessing of spending precious time with my mam and dad. Part of me was scared, because it was the first occasion as an adult I was effectively out of work for any extended period of time. The other part of me was thrilled to be able to support the people who had given me so much over my life. I didn't know it at the time, but the decision to act as a carer with Dad for Mam was one of the most important of my entire recovery journey.

Needless to say, Mam was thrilled. I would take them both to doctor's appointments, collect whatever medicines they needed, do the weekly shopping with Dad for them but, most of all, I'd simply make a cup of tea, then sit down and chat about family and local news. Often, I'd sit and talk with my mam, just holding her hand and chatting about old times.

At one point, her treatment required special injections into her stomach. I'm not the best with needles, and would never in a million years consider working as a nurse. But my mam needed me, and I went along to support her and do whatever she needed.

Sometimes I would sit and rub her feet to help with her circulation. Other times, we would sit and drink endless cups of tea and chat about family and local news. I started to lie down on the bed next to her to chat, something I had not done in many years. Those few months are today among the most prized memories of my entire life because, without even realising it, Mam and I stopped being mother and daughter and became great friends.

Those six months also saw the children call regularly to the Janesboro house and spend time with their grandparents. It was a tonic to see how much Mam and Dad revelled in the affection of their grandchildren. They seemed to draw strength from the next generation. For all the children – but especially for Jack and Sarah – it was special to feel such a valuable part of a large extended family.

When the children would arrive at Mam and Dad's home, they would invariably start colouring. Mam would join in and, though she never admitted it, she found colouring with the children very therapeutic. She would also sit and listen to all their stories from school and the clubs they were involved in.

Sometimes, Mam and Dad would fetch old letters and read them aloud to me. They revelled in pulling out memorabilia, like the old Munster rugby programmes from when Munster beat the All Blacks in 1978, or even Jason and Wayne's old altar boy outfits. Mam would also read out her favourite poetry; she was especially proud of her sister Bernadette's poems, which has been published and were framed on the wall in our kitchen. She would also ask me for news of the neighbours and the community and discuss local and national politics. Sadly, she was now dependent on a wheelchair if we had to leave the house. I could sense there were days when she was deeply frustrated at her inability to do the work around the house that she prided herself on for almost 50 years.

But, despite all our efforts, I felt Mam began to slowly distance herself from us. Almost imperceptibly, she seemed to grow smaller and frailer. She also started to drift to the fringes of conversations. Jason's killing had inflicted a lot of pain and suffering on her, and its toll was now apparent. Whereas once she would demand all the news, now she seemed to sit back and let others do the talking around her.

We were all thrilled when Sarah was honoured with a Limerick Garda Youth Award in November 2019 to honour her authoring *Noodle Loses Dad* and the time she devoted to reading her book to children's groups and charities working with vulnerable youngsters. It was a bright glimmer of pride and happiness in a time of worry for my mam and dad.

I wrote in my diary on New Year's Eve 2019 about how I hoped the year ahead would be better than the 12 months that just passed. I wrote that 'Everything about the future is uncertain – same dreams, fresh starts. But we have been blessed with so much love and support. A little love to yourself as we approach the New Year.'

Who could have guessed that 2020 would usher the world into a pandemic crisis not witnessed since the Spanish Flu of 1918? For my family, it also marked the beginning of a nightmare 18 months that ranked alongside August 2015 for anguish.

By October 2019, my mam had been repeatedly talking about how she wanted to see Spanish Point in Clare – the beloved holiday retreat of our childhood years. I think she viewed a trip there as a beacon of hope after her hospital stay and convalescence at home from her heart attacks.

So Dave and I organised a two-night stay at Bellbridge House Hotel for us and Mam and Dad that October. All we did was talk, eat mouth-watering food by the fireside and stare out at the wild Atlantic waves as they battered the rocky coastline.

I would get Mam settled and cosy in her wheelchair and take her for walks along the paths where, as children, she would play with us. Mam's eyes glittered with nostalgia as we walked past places associated with some of the happiest memories of our family. It was only later that I realised the significance of that short trip. It was Mam's last time viewing the Clare coastline she adored. It was also the last holiday she would ever have.

Christmas 2019 came and went with the same mix of festive joy and melancholy for those we had lost over recent years. We had 14 people for Christmas dinner, and both Mam and Dad revelled in the attention and the warmth of family surrounding them. We had no idea of what the new year was about to unleash on us all.

Because I was Mam's full-time carer, I was able to visit their home during the pandemic, but I was careful to ensure I wore a protective mask. Despite the regrets on both sides, the children were no longer able to visit their grandparents. But they would do jobs for them around the garden, such as cutting the grass – and my mam and dad would open their bedroom window and chat to them from a safe distance.

Mam and Dad had two amazing carers who came in each week to assist them. In my view, they were the unsung heroes of Ireland's response to the pandemic. Yet, despite our best efforts, it was clear that Mam and Dad were feeling the stress of being effectively trapped like prisoners in their own home.

The community did its best to help. There was an online community bingo, Mass was streamed and local businesses arranged for home deliveries of vital goods. My parents had been schooled in the wonders of online messaging services, and they spoke face-to-face each day with family members.

We were so strict about protection measures. Mam and Dad had cocooned for their own safety from a very early stage. They should have been safe. But, sadly, as so many families discovered, the virus was as implacable a foe as it was deadly. It was simply impossible to protect everyone.

On the evening of 11 April, Mam rang me to say she wasn't feeling well. I felt an instant sense of panic – and I don't think I imagined it when I detected concern in my mother's voice. Mam said she had a tightness in her chest, and was finding it difficult to breathe. While it may be hard to believe, I was almost praying it was a heart issue rather than the virus.

I have to admit I was terrified. Putting on my personal protective gown and face mask, I immediately went to my parents' home and checked on my mam. She was able to chat but complained about her breathing and her throat. I wanted to call for an ambulance, but Mam steadfastly refused. She did not want to go to the hospital. I applied a medicinal spray to her throat and, a short time later, she insisted she felt better.

However, the following morning, 12 April, she admitted she was still feeling unwell and I called for an ambulance. I felt the fear well up within me like a giant wave, but I fought it. I had to remain calm and composed for the sake of my parents. As we waited for the paramedics, I packed her bag and made sure she had nighties, underwear, slippers, a bathrobe, her favourite toiletries and some reading material. Above all, I made sure she had her phone with her with a charger, as I wasn't sure if she would be allowed visitors in the current Covid-19 control regime.

Mam's priority was that she had her Rosary beads and her prayer book. That's the kind of woman she was. Throughout the wait, she was calm and tried to chat to us – though it was clear that it wasn't easy for her because of her breathing.

When the ambulance pulled up outside our front gate, my dad was asked to wait in the kitchen – while he was beside himself with worry for his beloved Rita, medical professionals wanted to ensure he was protected as best as possible. Though my mam, God love her, did her best to appear brave, it was clear she was terrified as she watched them go to work in their full PPE.

The paramedics were lovely and extremely gentle with Mam. They lifted her onto a chair, tucked a blanket carefully around her and carried her downstairs. Then they brought her out to the ambulance and hoisted her inside. Throughout the entire process, they kept chatting to her in a bid to keep her calm and ease her concerns.

My mother had left her beloved family home for the last time, though we didn't know it then. Truth be told, I think I feared it that day. Some neighbours came to their doors and gestured towards us in support, some waving, while others blessed themselves. I have no doubt that their concern was mixed with relief that it wasn't their family facing the Covid-19 nightmare.

The ambulance swept away, heading the short distance

to UHL. My mam had left behind her family home, the house where she had raised her children, welcomed her grandchildren, cooked dinner every day for almost 50 years and built a proud, love-filled life. I stood at the back door of the ambulance as it prepared to depart and felt a sense of foreboding that, as the doors closed, they were also closing on my mother's life in Janesboro.

Mam was just over 48 hours in UHL when the dreaded diagnosis came in – she had tested positive for Covid-19. Because of pandemic control measures, no visitors were allowed at that time at any Irish hospital, medical clinic or nursing home.

It broke my heart not to be able to sit beside my mam, to hold her hand, to embrace her and offer her the comfort of physical presence. But we had the lifeline of her phone. Mam chatted every day with my dad, her children and her grandchildren.

The nursing staff – despite being run off their feet – were incredible. They made sure Mam's phone was charged, and they kept us informed about her progress. Despite her diagnosis, Mam was lucid, and her mind remained sharp. She loved any family or community news we were able to share, and her guiding light was the prospect of recovering sufficiently to be allowed home.

Her grandchildren were inspired in their efforts to make her feel loved, wanted and missed. Sarah performed a special song, which she posted online, and which my mam was able to view from her hospital bed. Her grandchildren – not to mention myself, Marilyn, Wayne and our other siblings – would ring Mam from just outside UHL. Mam couldn't leave her bed to look out the window to see us, but we wanted her to know we were as close as we could possibly get to where she was.

Mam's condition stabilised over the next week. By 22 April, she had had two negative Covid-19 tests, and her condition had improved slightly. Doctors decided she could be transferred to St John's Hospital. It was hoped her recovery would benefit from being away from the more frenetic environment of a busy acute hospital. When she was transferred, Mam's mind was sharp as a razor. She interpreted the transfer as her being prepared for her return home.

I bought her new pyjamas as well as other essentials she needed, I would pick up and drop back her washing – all triple bagged for safety and with all washing done while I was wearing gloves, full PPE and a face mask. Every time I was near the hospital, I rang Mam to let her know I was there and thinking of her.

We had tried to look on the bright side. I sent a text message to a niece after the 22 April transfer that read, 'Hiya love – Mam is in over ten days now and is coming out the other side and doing much better, thank God. She has just transferred to St John's. She told me she was talking to you all. Hope you are all well.'

The nights were the hardest. Having said goodbye to Mam after our evening chat, I would question myself each evening in the privacy of my bedroom – had I done enough for Mam and Dad? Could I have done things differently? Was I the kind of daughter they deserved?

Then came the worst possible news – Mam had developed pneumonia. That was what I had dreaded. Mam was still one hundred per cent focused, but doctors told me they were worried her body was slowly losing the fight – most especially her brave but damaged heart. She just didn't have the physical reserves left to win the fight that Covid-19 and now pneumonia had forced on her.

On 9 May, Mam was again gravely ill, and we all feared the worst. If Mam realised she was dying, she never said it outright. The doctors were honest with us, and I felt I owed honesty to my mam. You want to say the right things, you want to make the right decisions, but you also are trying to balance respect and honesty with sensitivity and compassion. Above all, I didn't want Mam to be upset or frightened.

The awful thing about a Covid-19 death was how isolated it kept people from their loved ones. Nurses, doctors, paramedics and care staff worked miracles – and did their best to ensure people never felt alone. There was no discrimination when it came to dying during the Covid-19 pandemic – everyone was isolated.

In her final days, it was apparent to all how frightened

my mam was. She had tremendous faith, and that helped her deal with her fear. But I could tell she was afraid. I found it overwhelming, because I was powerless to help. Mam was left navigating the final days of her life along with three other patients on a ward at St John's. There was very little privacy or intimacy – Mam said everyone she met was clothed from head to toe in PPE.

By this point, she was so weak that she wasn't able to mount a defence on our behalf – she admitted she missed us, hated being isolated from her family and longed for her home. There was no pretence or attempt at denial. I couldn't rub her feet to help her with her circulation, I couldn't bring her a cup of tea to cheer her up or even offer the comfort of taking her hand in mine.

There are times when death is not dignified. It can be slow, ruthless and painful to the point where the end is almost welcomed as a relief from over-long suffering. For Mam, she fought so hard for so long that, in the end, she had nothing left to fight with. All she was left with was mental anguish and physical suffering from the slow failure of her own frail body.

I got a call very early in the morning from the hospital to alert me that Mam's condition had significantly deteriorated. When I arrived, I was put into full PPE and ushered up to the ward, where the doctor called me aside to tell me to prepare for the worst. I stood in a corner on the corridor as nurses squeezed by in their PPE. The only sounds were the odd beep from a monitoring machine or a feeble 'Nurse' called out by a sick patient.

I had not seen my mother in several weeks – we had only had the Facetime chats when she was in UHL. As I entered her ward, I tried to hide the shock on my face. Mam had lost so much weight she appeared to be a fragile doll in the bed. But when we set eyes on each other we smiled and cried together. I couldn't touch or embrace her. All we wanted to do was to hold each other. 'Oh Tracey,' she whispered to me.

All I wanted to do was take my mother home so she could spend her final days in the place she loved more than any other on this earth. If she was going to die, I wanted her to die in a place of comfort and love. But the medical staff said it was out of the question. Mam had pneumonia and was too frail to be moved. It was also deemed too high a risk with Covid-19.

Miraculously, when I rang the hospital the following morning – my birthday – the staff nurse came on to say Mam was now doing well, she was out of bed and had even agreed to eat a little. I asked to visit, but as she had improved there was no way they were about to let me see her again.

I spent the afternoon with the kids, making get-well-soon cards with pictures glued on from each and every one of us. All the kids stuck their pictures with their Nana on them and wrote such beautiful messages of love.

We then had a Zoom call with my aunts and cousins from the UK, who were all concerned and in regular contact to check up on Mam. The only person missing from our family home was Mam. The remainder of that afternoon I spent dropping off groceries – when I came home that evening the kids had baked a cake from scratch, iced it and had written 'Happy Birthday' on it, and made tapas for my birthday.

I knew they were going to the extra effort to distract me from the worry of Mam's impending death. It was very touching, and I did my best not to weep, as I was feeling so fragile. We sat around the dining table and I felt comforted. Mam would normally have been in the middle, surrounded by us all, but for now I held to the knowledge she was safe in the hospital and still with us.

I had sent a text to Wayne and Marilyn: 'Just spoke to the hospital for an update from Doc – Mam is improving! The antibiotics are working, she's on new heart medication and it seems to be helping. She ate a little and took two steps. She's still seriously ill but is reacting well to the drugs. They said they were very concerned last week – those concerns are lessened with her responses today.'

The following day I checked in with the hospital and they said Mam was OK and had remained stable. I also spoke to Mam and she asked me to come to see her. I promised I would try – I felt I needed to go in, and practically begged the nursing staff. They relented and allowed me in. When I arrived, the doctor wanted to see me – he met with me in the corridor – Covid-19 gave no time for politeness or gentleness.

Everyone who was in those hospitals was under tremendous stress – from patients and medical staff to family members. Death seemed to be lurking everywhere. The doctor warned me that Mam was not getting better and that patients sometimes briefly rallied for whatever reason. It was like someone had taken a knitting needle to my balloon of hope. Mam may have rallied a little, but it was clear that the doctors felt her immediate prognosis hadn't changed.

The doctor looked at me with sympathy and said, 'Your mother's body is failing her, organ by organ, Tracey.' He said it in such a matter-of-fact way. I was grasping for even the slimmest scrap of hope, but there was none on offer. I could see the inevitability of what lay ahead in his eyes. I whispered, 'How long?' He replied that it could be days, but said she was a fighter so it could be longer.

He was right. Mam was a fighter and stubborn to her backbone. Her spirit was still strong, but it was slowly being betrayed by her exhausted body. It was during this visit that she gave me a gift I will cherish for the rest of my life. As we prepared to finish our evening chat, she paused and then told me, 'You were the best daughter.' I thanked her, and then somehow held things together until I left the room and collapsed into tears. It was during this visit that my mother liberated me from any burden I carried about decisions I had made. Not everyone in our family agreed during the preceding years of trauma with every difficult decision. Grief affects us at different stages, and some stay rooted in anger and feel helpless.

My mother told me I should stop trying to please everyone. She said she loved me and wanted me to keep fighting for what was right, for Jason, no matter what. Those precious moments were some of the most sacred in my life. My mother was exhausted, frightened and knew she was facing death. But she was still trying to care for me in her final hours. I promised there and then that I would do my best to honour her memory.

It was the hardest thing I ever had to do when the nurse gently told me it was time to go for the third time. Somewhere deep inside I knew I wouldn't see my mother alive again. I didn't want to go, but I had to. Surrounded by that hospital smell of antiseptic, combined with the odour of plastic from the PPE, I fought back tears and tried to stay brave for the brave little woman who watched me leave from her hospital bed.

The doctors and nurses at UHL and St John's were incredible, some of the true heroes of the pandemic in Ireland. At one point, a UHL nurse helped my mam set up a special Facetime contact with our family. I was on the call, along with Adam, Jack and Sarah. We chatted and then Sarah sang a special song for her gran. Mam was delighted – and, on the spur of the moment, I took a screenshot. She was smiling and wearing her grey dressing gown. It was the last normal conversation we had.

After that, Mam deteriorated fast, and could only really utter whispers when we rang her. Two days later, the doctors told us to inform the rest of the family that only brief visits of five minutes each would now be permitted – end-of-life patients were the only ones allowed visits from their loved ones.

Mam had somehow beaten Covid-19, but it had taken such a toll on her frail system that she just didn't have the strength to fight on anymore. By 15/16 May, we were told the end was near. She died in St John's Hospital on Sunday 17 May. My father was devastated. He had spent 61 years with his beloved Rita. The following day, all I could do was post a special tribute to my mam on social media. It was my way of coping, because I just couldn't deal with the avalanche of calls from friends, neighbours and supporters from all across the world who tried to contact me to express their sympathy.

I posted on both Facebook and Twitter that, 'My courageous, resilient, beautiful and kind mother, my biggest advocate, closed her eyes for the last time last night. Go gently into the good night and be enveloped in the loving arms awaiting you. RIP Rita Corbett 1939–2020.'

We decided that, for her death notice, we would use a photograph of Mam smiling and holding up a cup of tea in one of her finest bone China cups. It was an image that captured the very essence of my mam – happy, contented and the anchor of her entire family.

Later, I added a note to Facebook that summed up the devotion to each other my mam and dad shared.

> [Dad] spends the last moments of a lifetime [in] the only place he would want to be, holding the hand of his sweetheart with whom he shared over 60 years of marriage.
>
> Dad is fit as a fiddle and sharp as a tack. Almost the same as the woman he was going to visit in her place of Covid-19 aftercare. Rita's mind was razor-sharp – but her body was slowly failing her organ by organ.

Mam was the fulcrum of all our lives, and it broke my heart when we received the call from the nursing staff to say her final hours were upon her. Dad was brought to see her one final time, and it was heart-breaking. I was so moved by what had happened that day that, as my dad paid an emotional farewell to his beloved Rita, I wrote out my thoughts – as much a tribute to my mam as a form of therapy:

> A Covid-19 loss ... I closed my eyes last night as the edges of sleep beckoned. Your love is there surrounding me, I find its embers fiercely burning in my heart. I kiss

your cool papery cheek in my dream. Your soft hand gently rests in the clasp of mine. You are relishing the feeling of physical touch. You are scared and you want to come home but I am helpless.

I feel your delicate, fragile body weakened and limp in my arms as I hold you so close for the last time. They called to say, come visit – it is time. The last visit. It was the first since you were taken to your home of Covid-19 care so long ago.

They said I gave you strength to hold on – [your] vitals improved. We cried together, you and I, so hard when we held each other. You told me what a daughter needed to know from her mother. You lived another desperately lonely week. I wish you didn't, for to know and to have witnessed your isolating loneliness viscerally seared itself into my mind, scorching all my memories for so long.

Last night I dreamed of you – the real you. The lifetime of memories you helped create. I see you again for the first time in my mind sitting on the rock as the waves crash onto the beach. The wind whips your hair as you turn your face up to the sun and smile in contentment. I thought I had lost you – now, I know you are not just a Covid-19 death. You are every memory. You are love. You are at peace.

Once again, I was indebted to my cousin, Nuala Galvin, who worked so hard to shield me from the glare of the media as, yet again, I mourned the loss of a beloved pillar of my life. Nuala issued any statements that were required to the media and ensured our privacy was respected. She issued a beautiful tribute to my mam, which almost all the Irish newspapers subsequently printed:

Most of all, Rita loved her family unconditionally. She was such a good mother and grandmother. And so proud, she liked nothing more than to sing the praises of them all. Rita's family was her biggest achievement in life and losing Jason was her greatest sorrow. Rita told me she always felt Jason was with her and now they are together forever. There is some comfort in that. We love you and we will miss you. We hope you have finally found the peace you lost when Jason was stolen from you.

For as long as I can remember Rita has been in my life. She's my mother's best friend and sister. Her loss will be immeasurable to us all. But it does not compare to the loss felt by her husband John, her children, grandchildren and great-grandchildren.

Rita was warm, loving, soft, welcoming, compassionate, resilient and forgiving. She had the best smile – that lit up a room. Rita and I shared a love of watching *Home and Away*, and reading books. She loved Mills and Boon, maybe because she was a romantic and believed that love conquered all. Rita found great comfort and believed in her angels.

One of the most precious things that Covid-19 stole from us was the ability to harness the support of the community in mourning our loved ones. Because of infection controls, funerals had to be held in private. That vital communal outpouring of sympathy and support was no longer permitted. The only way people could show their support was by signing an online condolences form. Or by standing patiently by the roadside, all carefully socially distanced and often wearing masks, to pay a visible tribute to the person as they undertook their final physical journey.

Mam's funeral was staged with only immediate family members present. The arrangements were sensitively handled by Cross Funeral Directors and, as we expected, the friends and neighbours in Colbert Park in Janesboro paid a special roadside tribute to Mam, which brought tears to all our eyes. The funeral was so challenging. We were only allowed 12 people inside the church for her Requiem Mass. We couldn't embrace each other or offer any form of physical comfort or sympathy.

But the most awful part of the funeral was seeing what my heartbroken dad was faced with. He couldn't mourn the loss of the love of his life in the manner that had evolved in Ireland over generations. The morning after Mam died, I called to check on my dad when I spotted him getting dressed in his good clothes. I asked him what he was doing. He simply replied, 'I am going to be with your mother.'

He wanted to sit beside her, hold vigil in the funeral home and say his own goodbye after a lifetime spent together. I instantly knew that Dad wanted to spend as much time as possible with his love before the cremation. But he wouldn't be allowed to do so because of Covid-19 regulations – and it broke my heart to tell him.

It was so unfair that he never got to have his final goodbye with Rita. He didn't get to hold her hand or sit by her coffin and recall all the golden memories they had forged together over 61 years. It was nothing short of cruel what the pandemic had done to him and to countless other people across the world. It was the final indignity, the parting kick from that awful virus.

Instead, Dad had to sit in a crematorium two metres away from my sister and I, both flanking him, as he watched a short film about Mam before the curtains drew closed on their life together. The brief tribute ended with the strains of Dame Vera Lynn's 'We'll Meet Again'. It was nothing like the farewell they should have shared.

Tragically, the pandemic allowed no do-overs, no replacement tributes or no fixing of broken hearts. It was so wrong and compounded the loss that devastated loved ones had suffered. Mam and Dad had shared a lifetime of love and friendship. It wasn't how their story should have ended.

In a final gesture that my mam would heartily have approved of, we asked that instead of flowers mourners might donate to the Children's Grief Fund. It was a charity that was very close to Sarah's heart, and to which she had insisted a portion of the proceeds of her 'Boogawooga' book be donated.

Mam wanted to be buried with her son who had died before her. But Jason was buried with his wife in a double grave that had limited space. Dad wanted to be buried with his wife when he died. He decided the only option left was to have Mam cremated and interred with Jason and Mags – so that, when his own time came, they could be buried together.

So many things remind me of Mam. The smell of Oil of Olay moisturiser, a freshly brewed cup of tea and her walking stick still placed at the ready in the hallway of her home. It was only after she was gone that I began to fully appreciate all that she had brought to our lives.

My mother selflessly put aside all of her personal aspirations in life to put others first, especially her family. To her, the life of an 'Irish Mammy' wasn't just a duty, it was a life mission. She filled our lives with unquestioned love and, somewhat selfishly, we accepted it. Only when she was gone did we realise just what a fount of support, love and kindness she truly was.

She was clever, funny and hard-working. But whatever she had hoped to be in life besides being a mother she put aside for us. My mother's career was her children, and she gave us everything she possibly could. She looked after our children as we built our careers, she was a good sounding board in life's complicated situations and was a voracious reader.

When I worried about writing my first book, it was my mother and sister who told me it had to be done. When I've had to make some of the most difficult decisions in my life, my mother was the one who issued me my marching orders and told me no task was beyond me. In August 2015 it was my mother who sent me to the US with the simple instruction to bring Jason's children back to Ireland.

All she ever asked for was to be included in the lives of the family members she loved so dearly. When I would call to see Mam and Dad, if I brought a mini-lemon meringue for her, she was thrilled. My mam was always delighted if you thought of her. That was all the thanks she ever wanted for a lifetime of selfless love.

In the days after Mam's funeral, I struggled. I had a wellness plan. I had love and support from my family. But grief is a cunning foe and, once again, I started to regress and to slip back into the negative behaviours that had proved so destructive after Mags's death.

The most serious was falling off the wagon in terms of healthy eating. I suspect my family knew I was in a bad place and didn't want to make too big an issue over it. Within a few months, I had suddenly put on two stone, was feeling bad and struggling to find a balance in my life.

It didn't help that the spectre of the US murder appeal kept coming up with more documentaries and podcasts being released. It didn't matter if we participated or not, they still went ahead, so the pressure to speak up for Jason remained relentless. I realised the critical importance of the North Carolina Supreme Court decision and its implications, but part of me was missing my mam and worried about my dad. Focus was something I struggled to harness.

Fortunately, I stayed true to myself and began to return to my recovery programme. I returned to a healthy eating regimen and started chatting to my family and friends about how I felt. It made me feel balanced. There is something about knowing we are doing the right thing that offers an inner boost to the spirit. What is important is that, in the innermost parts of our psyche, we know we are trying our best.

All my life, the wild Clare coastline has been a place of childhood happiness and refuge. When I look at the Atlantic Ocean, I'm captivated by the wildness and fearlessness of nature. The sea reminds me of my mother – strong, bold and determined. Not surprisingly, I picked the Clare coastline to be the place where I honoured my mother's spirit – and said my own private farewell to her.

My mother was the personification of the 'Irish Mam'. She would do anything for her family, and especially her children.

She went without to ensure we had the things in life we needed – even if, at times, we felt like we didn't deserve them. Her love was all-powerful and unconditional.

When my mam got mad at you for some misdemeanour, you were left feeling just inches tall. But we also knew without question that she loved us. She was the most amazing, strong and courageous woman you could ever know.

She got up early in the morning if we had an early start just to make sure we were OK and that we had a good breakfast to start the day. She would wait up late at night to ensure we got home safe.

Mam taught me some of life's most valuable lessons – things I couldn't have learned from anyone else. The most priceless lessons were learned from her examples of hard work, selflessness and devotion. She was the anchor of our family and a woman who valued character and integrity above everything else. If my mam said she was proud of you, it was like winning the Nobel Prize. My mother was a tough taskmaster, and compliments weren't dished out lightly – you had to earn them.

For some people, there is an inevitability about raising our loved ones up a little when they pass away. We amplify their good points and ignore their failings. It is a common theme that many attend funerals where the eulogy depicts someone on a par with Jesus Christ. The picture painted may be impressive and even inspiring, but, in many cases, it bears little or no resemblance to the person involved. A wit once joked after sitting through a lengthy eulogy at an Irish funeral that he feared he was at the wrong Mass, because the glowing description of the deceased bore little resemblance to the man he had known.

I don't grieve for any glorified version of my mam. She was sweet, generous, kind and loving. But she was also stubborn, set in her ways and a woman who fiercely defended her family, just like us all. The woman I mourn is the mother I knew – she wasn't perfect in human terms. No one ever is. But she was perfect to us, and the best mother anyone could be blessed with.

Probably the hardest thing to reconcile was what Covid-19 did to all our elderly, not just my mother. The pandemic involved the decimation of our older community. It also put on full display the remarkable fortitude of families and the lengths people will go to shield and protect their loved ones – the bravery, strength of mind, fortitude and determination to get loved ones through the pandemic. As a nation, our collective support of each other, solidarity and common purpose helped save so many lives. Sadly, my mam and so many others did not live to tell the tale and marvel at how ordinary people rallied to help each other.

In the months after her death, I found it was the small things that would trip me up. My mother had for decades looked after the remembrance notices for our family. These were the notes put in the local Limerick newspapers to mark the anniversaries of lost relatives. I also discovered that the responsibility for the family graves was now mine.

But I found it impossible with all that was going on in my life to remember to do all these little things such as remembrance notices. Mam did them quietly and without fuss. Letting go of them just broke me up. It was as if a tangible link with my mam had been severed. It was also another reminder of how many things she had done to keep our family connected, united and in touch with our history.

REMINDER

We only fail in life when we stop trying. Anyone can suffer losses, setbacks, injustice and even cruelty. I'm not saying life is easy. But I truly believe we are defined not by our triumphs but rather by how we face our setbacks – how we pick ourselves up, dust ourselves down and start anew at life.

10

LOVE IS YOUR SECRET WEAPON

There are days when, from the deep recesses of my memory or soul, old feelings of loss resurface. At times, they are so raw and powerful that they threaten to overwhelm my initial coping mechanisms. But successive losses, and years spent in what I like to call self-recovery, have taught me not to panic.

As I've said before, grief isn't linear; it isn't predictable, and its strength comes in waves, with the peaks often influenced by external factors and events, such as anniversaries, coincidences, places and the like. I have learned to utilise my full array of coping mechanisms – if one doesn't work, I turn to another and so on until the wave of emotions associated with the grief memory begins to ebb.

The point is that it is OK to feel upset. We can't feel normal or upbeat all the time. It is only natural for us to react emotionally to certain circumstances in life, even years after a loss – after all, it is what makes us human. I've often found myself dancing around the kitchen with the children when a great song comes on the radio, something which I would never have done pre-grief. Today, I grasp every opportunity for joy that I can, because I know it can prove so fleeting.

Sometimes I have to resort to special steps to cope with these emotions and to protect the hard-won stability of my life. It helps that I work hard at my recovery plan and try to keep my positivity reserves regularly topped up in case of such setbacks.

There are occasions when it can be challenging to keep things on an even keel. Usually, the worst times are when memories of Mags, Jason, Mam, Kevin and others collide and combine. The trigger can be a place, an anniversary, a photograph or even a song on the car radio. Garth Brooks once announced he was playing a series of concerts in Ireland, and this triggered such poignant memories of youth, freedom, love and happiness from times past. So many of his songs are part of Jason and Mags's life. It reminded me of their excitement at going to see him play live in 1997. These memories can be very emotional and moving, but I welcome them now with gladness. We have to balance the darkness of loss and pain in our lives. Not surprisingly, the challenging times usually occur when something also has happened in my life that has left me feeling hurt, tired or vulnerable.

The North Carolina Supreme Court decision to uphold Molly and Tom Martens' appeal against the second-degree murder conviction over Jason's death was one of those times. The ruling in March 2021 – by a wafer-thin verdict of four to three of the appellate judges – was utterly devastating, not just for me but for our entire family. The sheer power held by individuals cannot be underestimated. I prayed those judges would have enough evidence of fact in their review to make the right decision – a decision that would severely impact our family's way of life. We had spent so many hard-won painful days, nights, weeks and months striving for balance in our lives and a way to live again without our loved ones.

It wasn't just that the justice we had worked so hard to achieve was thrown out, but an even more bitter pill to swallow was the fact that we all knew what lay in front of us with a retrial. Jack and Sarah had lived almost half their lives under the shadow of the American justice system. They deserved to live their lives instead of having them pushed back into therapy and support weighted down by a world they should have no knowledge of. It's impossible to convey or explain the effect this can have on a parent. That sheer sense of powerlessness. The feelings of futility at that moment of hard-won battles that were now apparently lost.

It felt as if we were caught in some cruel real-life version of Snakes and Ladders. Just when we seemed to have some finality on the horizon in front of us, we were catapulted straight back to square one, irrespective of all the pain and suffering it entailed. I was determined to fight with every ounce of courage in my being for a retrial. But I had to acknowledge that I needed time and space to allow myself to process and come to terms with the implications that this decision made over in America would have on our lives. There was the psychological impact and the practical consequences, such as our choice to move house. Jack had to leave his private school, as the pressure was too much. The best-laid plans imploded again.

These I had to deal with before we were ready for the next step. But there was no way on earth I was going to allow two murderers to escape justice for taking my brother's life. Always give yourself time to process events, especially before making life-altering decisions – reflect, consider, consult and always give yourself time.

From the very core of my being I knew I would never give up the fight for justice. But, at the same time, I dreaded it, because the first trial had effectively consumed two years of our lives. Would a retrial now consume another couple of years? The original trial process had left us emotionally battered and bruised – and we hadn't known what was coming.

Now we knew what a retrial would involve, and that made it ten times worse. So much had not been made public in 2017, as the children hadn't given evidence. With a new trial, the world would know precisely what Molly Martens was capable of, and I firmly believe a murder conviction will be returned.

I am a mother first and foremost, and it brings me so much heartache and so many sleepless nights that Molly Martens so publicly exploited the two children to try to escape a murder conviction. I can't protect Jason, but I will do what is right for my children. The worst thing is she knows what will now be made public. But a few years of freedom before returning to prison meant more to her than the lives of the children she professed to love as her own.

The Martens' appeal had effectively been won on the basis of statements from Jack and Sarah not being admitted to the original July/August 2017 trial. But not only would their statements now be included in a retrial but the children may very well be asked to give evidence. The original trial had lasted five weeks, but the retrial could, at least in theory, extend to seven weeks or even more.

The murder convictions being overturned, the battle to secure a US retrial and then the Covid-19 pandemic which claimed the life of my mam almost seemed to fall as orchestrated blows that left me reeling.

I practised mindfulness daily, I took time out for exercise, I was careful with my diet, I was in regular contact with my counsellor, and I held on for dear life to positives such as family outings and events with the children. I focused on extracting every bit of joy possible from each day. But I still found myself wilting under the hammer blows of negativity. There were days when it felt as if I was trying to hold back the tide with a bucket and shovel. There were days when I got the children up and dropped them to school only to return home, crawl into bed and pull the covers over my head. Any ordinary human being would have felt exhausted and disheartened.

Deep within, I could feel all the old fears and anxieties bubbling back to the surface. I knew I had to disconnect – to somehow keep the priorities of my day firmly within my day. It was time to keep it simple, to put one foot in front of the other and deal with the tasks of the day, and not get drawn into the frustration and stresses of the future, most of which I was powerless to influence at that point.

Acknowledging that I had no control over events and being able to disconnect from those negative things was critical to achieving the calm and balance I needed to regain control over my life. In achieving that, the children were absolutely essential. Just when I found myself wavering over some new setback or some fear about the retrial process, I drew strength from seeing how the children had bounced back from setbacks greater than any I had suffered.

As always, Clare was my place of refuge, my haven from the stresses of the world. It is the crucible of the most cherished times of my childhood and the most warming, embracing memories of the people I have loved most on this earth. When old pain threatened to overwhelm me, I learned to take special steps to cope with the challenges involved. I realised it was OK to feel afraid. But it was also perfectly acceptable for me to do things and go to places that helped me cope and made me feel a physical connection to the positives of my life.

One step I have developed is to visit an old sea well in Clare, past Liscannor. Over the decades, it has developed into a place of pilgrimage for those seeking solace and comfort. There is something about the place; I can best describe it as a special connection to nature. For me, it is a place of calm and a spiritual haven. When I feel the old spirits are restless – particularly when memories of my mam spring powerfully back – I head here.

I came to the well one blustery day in August 2021. It was a time when I was feeling particularly low. I was missing my mam. The previous 12 months had been nothing short of a nightmare for us: first the ruling by the North Carolina Court of Appeals in favour of Tom and Molly, then the Covid-19 pandemic bringing the world to a standstill, having to watch Mam succumb slowly before our eyes and then enduring the nightmare of having the North Carolina Supreme Court overturn the murder conviction and allow my brother's killers to walk free from prison. It was one hammer blow after another. Now, I had to face the retrial without the rock of support that was my mother.

It was as if Jason's memory was being mocked. My mam, the person I would turn to first for comfort and advice throughout my life, was no longer there. A huge rock of support had been wrenched from my life. Worse still, the two people who had taken my brother's life and lied to destroy his good name were back in their old lives – and Molly was apparently enjoying a coast-to-coast holiday in the US and having pictures of herself regularly put up on social media.

That August day the Clare holy well was eerily peaceful among the memories of the dead. The well was decked out in Rosary beads, photographs, handwritten notes, Post-its, poems, tokens and candles left by hundreds of visitors over the months and years. A quick study revealed they had been left by people from all over the world – all seeking comfort and solace from grief at this rugged place on the wild edge of Europe.

In a way, all the heartache of the world was focused on this little cave overlooking Liscannor and located in one of the most beautiful places on earth, just before the Cliffs of Moher. When I came here, I was reminded that while this is a place associated with death and grief, it is also a precious shrine to loved ones.

It is worth noting that all the messages left here are of cherished memories. That a devoted husband has not been forgotten. That a partner still loves his lost wife. That parents think of their dead child every moment of every day. In a way, this place is a sacred repository of treasured memories. When

I walk here, I realise I am not the only person struggling to make sense of grief and trying to escape the feeling that you are trapped in your own painful version of Groundhog Day. I am not the only person to have to live on with a broken heart. When I'm here, I don't feel so alone – as if there is a solidarity of grief out there.

Despite everything that has happened, I know I have a lot to live for. I love and am loved. That Clare well is a reminder to me to show love in my life on a daily basis. Care for those you love, don't be afraid to tell them what they mean to you. Make every single moment of your life count. Never let a row or a dispute keep you away from those you love. Each day, live your life so you don't have regrets. I really hope you find a way to fall in love with your life again after a bereavement. Don't just live – have a life.

When Mam died, my only regret was that she was gone. I had given her every possible moment of my time. I was there for her when she needed me most – and you have no idea what a comforting thought that was. For me, one of the most important totems on the recovery road is to use your time wisely, and to focus it on those you love. Don't waste it on futile anger or material things that offer cold comfort in times of loss.

Try to avoid nastiness, be scrupulously honest with yourself and your loved ones, don't hesitate to ask for forgiveness if you've done something wrong, show kindness to someone when you can, talk to those you love each day, even if it is just for a minute. Never, ever forget that today is the best day of your life – because it will never be repeated.

Love is the secret weapon we all have. When you consider your life, love is what drives us all. To lose a loved one is one of the most excruciating experiences in life. But to lose a loved one amid regret is vastly worse. It can haunt us for years. Grief over the loss of a loved one will, over time, crystallise into cherished memories of having had them in our lives. One of the most painful parts of grief for me is what I call the space of No Man's Land. For me it is something that occurred with each loss in my life. I would become disconnected from the positive feelings and beautiful memories and be left with only the pain of loss. I was unable to tap into any of the sounds, conversations and memories that helped recall the wonderful person who had been lost. It was only the negative that swirled around me.

Peace and healing only came when I forced myself to focus on the positive. If you have loved with all your heart and made time for those who you care about, there is nothing to tarnish or crack those precious memories.

My grief was eventually eased by the knowledge that I couldn't have loved Jason, Mam, Mags and so many others any more than I did; I always let them know how much they meant to me. In my life, I was always reminding these people that I cared, telling them, 'I love you', 'I am so proud of you',

'I'm sorry I hurt you' and 'Thanks for being there for me.' In my life I tried to display my love through actions: an embrace, a kiss or a simple pat on the shoulder. But I believe words are also important. You can never tell someone you care about that you love them too many times.

So while I regretted losing them, I had no regrets over how I loved them all when they were alive. To be honest, I don't know how I would have coped trying to balance grief with the regret over losing someone while on bad terms or not having told someone how much they meant to me. Dave has often asked me, 'Why do you reach out? They need to be the ones coming to you apologising.' I always have the same answer. I need to be true to myself, and if I open the door, I am taking responsibility for myself. Equally, I keep that door firmly closed if I feel it's going to be toxic for me or my family.

One story really struck home for me. I read about how Princess Mako agreed to renounce her royal status in Japan to marry a commoner, Kei Komuro, whom she had met in university. They married despite public disapproval and attempts by the powerful Japanese press to oppose the match. It got so bad that Kei Komuro even moved to study in the US, but the couple stayed in contact online and by telephone. They eventually married in Japan in October 2021 and signalled their intention to live in New York for the early years of their marriage.

Princess Mako explained her choice as being quite simple. 'Kei is irreplaceable for me. For us, marriage is a necessary choice to live while cherishing our hearts.' For his part, Mr Komuro said he couldn't imagine a life without his beloved girlfriend of eight years. 'I love Mako. I want to spend the only life I have with the one I love.' There is a lesson in that for all of us.

We all need constant reminders that time is the most precious commodity we have. It cannot be purchased with gold, silver or Bitcoin. But it can be wasted all too easily. I wasted too many hours and days wallowing in self-pity and sadness. Yet devoting time to proper grieving is not wasting it. Rather it is investing in a happier, more contented future, when we have processed our loss and slowly learned to live with it. The trick is to know the difference.

There is a strange comfort to be drawn from the realisation that none of us will make it out of this world alive. There is no escape, so why waste precious time trying to find one? What we leave behind is our legacy in terms of our family, the lives we have touched and what we have tried to achieve to make the world a better place. That's what we should devote our time to.

Our actions define our legacy. In a way, our legacy is what offers us a form of immortality, by placing us within the hallowed halls of memory. As long as we live in the memory of those we have loved and have helped during our lifetime, we are never forgotten and never truly gone. When we grieve, we accomplish that task for others.

To that end, I now try to use my time wisely. I undertook a course by the Buddhist nun, Pema Chödrön, called 'The Heart of the Matter'. It essentially marked another development stage in my counselling and inner growth. Each book I read led me to make discoveries about myself and helped me cope with the challenges I faced, particularly in relation to the US appeal process and the appalling realisation that our family had to face the prospect of a full retrial for Jason's killers.

I also decided to undertake another training programme called the Wellness Recovery Action Plan (WRAP). This was a global group developed from the writings of Mary Ellen Copeland. She was an American woman who suffered from anxiety, depression and mood swings. In 1997, she helped organise an eight-day event in Vermont that was attended by several dozen people who had battled the same issues, and who felt they could help each other with their recovery.

Some who attended were battling anxiety issues triggered by personal trauma. Others had lives plagued by depression. Several who attended had spent years in psychiatric institutions. Mary Ellen had grown disillusioned with the psychiatric establishment of that time and its reliance on medication-focused treatment that prioritised managing her illness rather than focusing on her return to health. The symptoms were treated as far more important than the underlying causes.

She conducted a survey among her peers, and it identified five key concepts to a successful recovery – hope, personal responsibility, education, self-advocacy and support. After Mary Ellen led the eight-day support event in Vermont it sparked a global adoption of similar wellness events.

I instantly identified with WRAP's five recovery keys. Although I didn't realise it, I had essentially gravitated towards those same things in my own life as I got better. Human beings are happiest and most fulfilled when we are working towards something – from a life goal to a career challenge or a recovery plan. There is nothing worse in life than drift.

There is something comforting, rewarding and empowering about the realisation that we are delivering on our potential. To do this, we need to push our limits – to stretch and expand beyond the invisible box we sometimes lock ourselves into.

We have to open ourselves up to new ideas, new experiences and new learning techniques. Ten years ago I'd have laughed if you'd suggested I would go on a wellness retreat. Instead, my priority would have been a city break or a rugby weekend overseas, complete with nice meals and plenty of chilled Prosecco. I would still love that, but people change, and so do our priorities.

My priority today is feeling better in life and discovering more about the inner person whose strength I had caught glimpses of throughout the North Carolina trial process and the various tragedies I'd been faced with. I was fascinated with the inner me – what my potential was and what made me tick. We are capable of so much more than we give ourselves credit for.

Truth was, I wanted to be the star of my own life – as every single one of us should. But how do you achieve that if you harbour doubts about the person you really are, the capabilities you have and the vulnerabilities you need to guard against? If I don't believe in myself then how can someone else?

I had reached the point in my life – or my recovery, if you prefer – where I needed to challenge not just myself but life. Challenging life itself may seem like a tall order. But what I discovered is that by challenging myself, by changing Tracey, by becoming the best version of me I possibly could – I did slowly begin to change my life. Because other people noticed and were curious about what I had done.

They watched a woman who would never challenge the status quo suddenly voice strong opinions about equality, intolerance and social disadvantage. My first job as a teenager was on the factory floor. But I became chief executive of an operation that had 160 staff. From being a woman who half expected to be told what to do by my male colleagues, I became a boss who confidently ran a workforce of men and women. It was a workforce I respected greatly, and many became some of my greatest allies in life.

I took on the 'haters' without having to engage in hate myself. From being a bystander in life, I got involved and decided, in my own small way, to try to make a difference. People saw someone like themselves suffer devastating losses and yet recover to walk tall and be the best version of themselves possible. They saw a woman from an ordinary working-class background who was a teenage mother go back to education while holding down a job. I learned not to be afraid to try new things, to set ambitious goals and to reach for the stars both for myself and for those I love.

I'm proud to say that by working to change myself, I have helped others start on their own journeys of change. It was one of the 'light bulb moments' in my life to discover that by helping others from the hard-won experience of grief I had gone through, I actually helped myself. When I gave someone in grief my time and I saw them benefit from it in some small way, I felt a surge of satisfaction. Slowly, as I changed, and as the people I helped changed, so the world itself slowly changed for me. I drew tremendous strength from that realisation. Because I must never forget that the very first concept in recovery is hope.

REMINDER

Love is your healing agent – it is the long-term antidote to grief, pain and anger. If we open ourselves up to love – whether it be a cherished memory of a lost loved one, engaging in a treasured life activity or contributing in some way to the good of our community – we help protect ourselves from all the negative emotions that loss can throw at us.

11

TIME IS OUR MOST PRICELESS TREASURE – SO GET BUSY LIVING

Silence can be deemed to be approval. There are times in life when you think that by remaining silent you keep yourself safe from conflict or confrontation. We think that silence is the safer, more prudent course. In fact, I have discovered that the opposite is the case. In life, yes, silence can sometimes be a more effective form of communication than speech. However, by not having the courage to speak out about what we believe in, what benefits us and what we oppose, we empower those whose views may ultimately do us harm.

Remember that sometimes we may be the only lighthouse that people see before they hit the rocks. One of my favourite quotes is from Morgan Harper Nichols, who said: 'Tell the story of the mountain you climbed – it could become a page in someone else's survival guide.'

The lesson I learned in life is that I have to be true to myself. If I feel strongly about something, I owe it to myself to speak up about it – even if it doesn't make me popular in the room at that particular time. Yes, there are some things that are best left unsaid. But not when it comes to matters of principle, family, justice, care and compassion.

I had to stop waiting for the world to save me. Over the years I became convinced that I was put on this earth for a reason. I had to learn the hard way that what you get out of the world is a direct reflection of what you are prepared to put into it. That was one of the lessons my brother Jason taught me.

My life threatened to go careening off the tracks until I found my 'brave'. It is alright to be wounded, diminished and uncertain in life at times. Grief can do that to you. Those are the times in life when we most need our anchors – faith, family, self-belief and our small routines. None of us can live in fear. At least not for long.

One example is that I was once a terrible traveller. It was all rooted in fear. I was scared of planes, boats and even long car journeys. While I am not totally over it – what individual who sits on an aircraft for a long-haul flight over the vast expanses of ocean isn't apprehensive? – I no longer let it impact my life or restrict my desire to see new places.

The scale of change is borne out by the fact that, several years ago, I was on holiday in Florida when Sarah insisted that we both get the same kind of smartphone cases.

Inscribed on each was the word 'Wanderlust'. It made me immensely proud to realise how my daughter viewed me. For me, it was a milestone achievement that the young woman once nervous about even a flight to the UK was now deemed a global traveller. For Sarah, I see it as an affirmation of a bright, talented and brave young woman about to explore this remarkable world.

There are times when you will disappoint people in life. It is an inevitable consequence of being human. We all make mistakes. The key is to recognise our mistakes, learn from them and move onwards and upwards. The ability to realise we have made a mistake, to own up to it and, if necessary, to apologise for it is the mark of a strong human being. To be truthful, I learned more from the mistakes I made in life than I ever did from my successes.

But the most critical thing of all is not to disappoint yourself – don't let a mistake trigger such fear that you allow it to define you. Each of us had dreams in our teenage years of who we wanted to be and what we wanted to do. Those dreams change with years but they never vanish. Grief forces you to re-evaluate your life. Though I didn't realise it at the time, I had settled in my life. I thought those dreams were for others, people I thought were more deserving, more special and more gifted than me. My recovery was rooted in looking deep within myself, discovering my dreams and deciding to live my life trying to make them come true.

So do what's right for you, even when it is the hardest thing you have ever faced. Let go of the loss, even when it hurts to do so. Face your fears with honesty – it is the most powerful defence you have. There are times when it is not going to be easy. I won't pretend there aren't days when even tears won't be enough.

Remember that while we are living there is someone out there each minute somewhere in the world who is taking their final breath from cancer, Covid-19, a car crash, a pulmonary aneurysm, asthma or the aftermath of violence. That person would give anything to do what you are able to do right now – go out and live.

It is OK to be afraid. If you've spent 50 years with someone as a cherished partner and they have passed, it isn't going to be easy. There would be something wrong if it was. At times, grief over the loss of a loved one can resemble having lost part of yourself. Recovering from that can take time. So be gentle and kind to yourself.

We owe it to ourselves and to those we loved to live on. New experiences are likely going to be more daunting than exciting. There will be times when you only want to sit in your living room, pull the shades and be alone. That is perfectly OK for a time. But only for a time. Because life isn't lived alone on our own personal island of grief.

Ask yourself this – would your loved one want you to hide from life, or would they want you to honour them by going out and living? Would you not want the same for them? I'm not saying you should join a glee club in the weeks and months after having lost a loved one. But if you are struggling, why not try a grief group? Or join an activity linked with your church? Or get involved in something you enjoy, whether it is golf, hillwalking, a choir or a history club. Do something that takes you out of solitude and puts you in the middle of other human beings. Don't quit if you feel uncomfortable after the first outing. Give it time.

No one can make the choices for us. It is hard and it will hurt, but if you try you will remain true to yourself and your loved one. Isn't that truly what you want? I tried to hide from life for a time – I wallowed in despair, and it was brutal. I drank copiously from the pity pot and the wine bottle. In the end, not only did I feel I was letting myself down but I was disappointing the people I loved most.

Seize the day. Go do the things you kept putting off until tomorrow. Get help if you need it. But get active in life and dedicate it to the person you lost. Live the best version of your life in their name.

Trust me, because I have walked both roads, and I can promise you that one hour properly lived is worth years of regret-filled, half-lived days. Live your day as if there will be no tomorrow. Don't be like me and wait 30 years to discover this truth about the potential of life. If I can give you one gift from this book let it be this – don't waste a single year of your life before you learn that today is the day that you should do whatever you want to do for yourself, for your loved ones and for all those you care about.

I was blessed with a great family that I love and am loved by. I didn't waste any of my time when it came to love – and that was the greatest kick-start to recovery I had. The sands of time swirl past relentlessly. Yesterday is history and we don't know what tomorrow holds for us, but today is where the true riches of life are to be found.

There is a lot of wisdom in the old phrase that the greater the love, the greater the loss. But never underestimate the capacity of the human spirit to recover, to renew and to re-energise for the future.

May I wish you well on your grief journey. I hope my story has been of help and, if even one of you has found some comfort in these pages, then it will have been worthwhile.

What I can tell you for certain is that there is no greater way of honouring those you have loved than to embrace life and live each day to its maximum possible degree. Try to live in the 'now'; don't prejudge a day or its experiences. The aim is to live each day, not just to endure it and drag ourselves through it. If we bring the anxiety and fear of tomorrow into today, all we do is spoil any joy the present moment has to offer.

There will be days when it won't be easy, but I promise you that, no matter the pain of working to recover from grief and heartache, it will all be worthwhile in the long run.

Never forget that you are not alone, and that there is help out there if you only have the courage to ask for it. You are the director of your own life. How the story goes is entirely up to you. In my case, I felt I owed it to those I loved and lost to extract the maximum amount of life from each and every day. What better way to honour them than to honour life itself?

REMINDER

Don't lose sight of what is precious in your life, and nothing is more valuable than time. So don't waste it. Get out and make the most of every single day that you are blessed with. That lesson applies to every single human being on our planet – so you are not alone.

GRIEF EXERCISES

f I have learned one thing from all I have gone through it is that negative, destructive grief loves nothing more than idleness, laziness and paralysis. And I'm not talking about quiet moments for self-reflection or mindfulness, which are essential to our long-term welfare and recovery from grief.

No, I'm talking about prolonged periods where we wallow in our sadness, loss and pain to the exclusion of everything positive and healing in our lives. The longer we wallow in our grief, the darker our place in life seems to become. The worse we seem to feel, the more we bury ourselves in pain and suffering, isolating ourselves all the while from life and those who love us. It is a very damaging cycle.

My grief journey taught me that, when I was ready, doing practical things helped me – a bit like how pulling back the curtains instantly brightens a room. A series of exercises were recommended to me by multiple friends and experts – each designed for a specific phase of my recovery.

They are designed to help us step back into the light, to remind us how precious life is, that each of us has value, that we have a purpose on earth and that the best way we can honour those we have loved and lost is to embrace life in their name. Those who loved us would want us to be happy in the years we have left.

Do *not* attempt all these exercises at once. Take them slowly, and I'd suggest attempting them in order. It is very important that you take your time when doing them. If you feel you are not ready for them, simply pause and come back to them when you are more comfortable. Feel free to do an exercise over again if it helps.

Grief impacts each of us individually and at different paces. There is no time limit for these exercises, and there are no right or wrong ways to undertake them. They are designed to shake you out of your torpor, to get positivity in your life and to help you process your grief. I wish you the relief that I got from doing them.

1. Recognise the change

One of the most beneficial things I'd like to pass along is a simple exercise in helping to understand the impact of trauma and grief on our lives. Take a crisp sheet of A4 paper. Now, just crumple that piece of paper – scrunch it up and let it sit on your table. It may unfurl ever so slightly, but it will not automatically go back to its original form. It has been transformed forever by an external force.

Essentially that is what your body and mind are like after grief or trauma, so many jagged edges and creases, in no particular pattern. The scrunching or loss has left that piece of paper unrecognisable from what it looked like just a few seconds before – the pristine, crease-free sheet of paper has been changed utterly.

But if you carefully flatten it with the palm of your hand on a hard surface, repeatedly smoothing and pressing it, it will again begin to resemble a flat sheet of paper, albeit one with creases and marks. Leave it under the weight of several books overnight and it will flatten still further.

Human beings are the same after grief – it is how we flatten or work out the marks grief has left on our lives that is the key to recovery.

2. Write a gratitude list

Get a pen and a copybook. On the left margin, write numbers from one to 20 – one number for each line on the page. Now write out on each line something you are grateful for in life – just a few words will suffice. Things like 'my family', 'my health', 'my job', 'my friends', 'my interests', etc.

If you manage to fill the page without thinking too much about it, you are indeed truly blessed and in touch with your inner gratitude. But the truth is that, even if you struggle at the start in compiling the list, you have a lot to be grateful for if you think long and hard about it.

Even if you think you have problems with the big items on most people's lists – such as family or health – there are other simpler gratitude issues that you can list. Do you have food in the fridge? Do you have a roof over your head? Do you have a clean change of clothes for tomorrow? Are you able to walk to a park or riverbank or a hill overlooking a city and watch the glory of a sunset? Can you sit and listen to your favourite album?

You may take these things for granted, but remember that for some people these are things that are impossible, not things that are routinely detailed on a gratitude list.

In isolation, our problems may seem like the worst in the world. Sometimes looking outside yourself helps us to reflect and find meaning again. If we engage with others, we realise that everyone on the planet has problems. Sometimes, if we consider it, others may be battling problems that dwarf ours. Find what has meaning to you now and use it to make the decision to reshape your life.

3. Create a grief ritual

A grief ritual can be a very helpful way of beginning the process of letting go. Instead of hiding from your loss, you slowly begin to face it – and prepare the ground for processing your grief and resuming your life. Grief rituals are also very useful aids during challenging times when losses are most keenly felt, such as Christmas, birthdays, anniversaries, etc.

The ritual can be as simple or as complex as you like – but it is best to keep it straightforward. One positive option is to do something in your loved one's name for Christmas or on their anniversary – by doing so you associate their name and memory with something that helps others and makes you feel good. You could do something for a charity in their name or agree to a sponsored walk in their memory. In some cases, people have established major annual fundraisers in the names of lost loved ones.

If that sounds too daunting, why not visit their favourite church or place, say a prayer there or light a candle in their memory. Some people also find it useful during such grief ritual visits to recall a special story about their loved one focused on an event surrounding that day.

4. Lean on others

One of the most destructive aspects of grief is that it tries to isolate us. Feeling lonely after a loss is perfectly understandable, so how on earth will we feel better if we shut ourselves off from others?

On our own, we can be vulnerable. There are times it is perfectly fine to grieve alone – in fact, there are occasions when leaning into your grief on your own is very important. But there are also times when we need others. This exercise aims to tackle that.

Commit to a social activity and set a date for doing so. This can be as big or as small as you like. If you're feeling fragile, pick up the phone, ring a friend and ask to meet for coffee and a meal. Or ask to meet for a game of golf or a walk on the beach, or go to a GAA or soccer match together. If your friend asks to meet again, commit to doing so – don't fudge. This is how we begin to re-engage with life and ensure we don't isolate ourselves.

If you are feeling a bit stronger, get involved in a social activity or re-join a club you were once part of. It could be a choir, a hillwalking club, a historical society, a camera club, a church group or a book club. But it *must* have face-to-face interactions – dealing with remote connections is not going to work.

5. Be in nature

There is power, solace and inspiration to be drawn from nature – so why not avail of it? It may also help to expose yourself to the seasons that reflect nature's own cycle of life.

Pick your favourite place – it doesn't matter if it is a city park, a riverside walk, a stunning stretch of coastline or the most windswept mountain. Go there and, if you like, bring a flask with a hot drink or some sandwiches. If you have a mobile phone, switch it to silent until you're on your way home.

Find a quiet spot where you can sit and savour the beauty of nature that surrounds you. Close your eyes and listen to the sounds you can hear – try to identify each and every one, from the rustle of the wind to the bird song and the chirping of insects in the grass. Take your time and don't rush.

Now, open your eyes and consider the awesome beauty that you are part of. Look up and watch the clouds scurrying overhead or the wind rustling the leaves or whipping up the waves. If there are animals nearby, pause to watch them. Picture the countryside and think about what makes this place so special for you. Now realise that you are part of this magnificent world as much as the birds, the insects, the clouds and the waves. Just as they have a purpose in life, so do you.

6. *Write a letter*

This is an exercise that is mostly used with children to help them with grief but, if I'm honest, I've found it very useful myself, so I think adults can benefit from it just as well as youngsters.

Take a sheet of paper and write a letter to your lost loved one. The aim should be to compose a goodbye letter. It is perfectly fine to say how much you loved them, what they meant to you and how difficult you have found life without them. Make sure to include the golden memories you have of them.

It is OK to pause the process if you get upset, and there is no limit to how long the letter can be. But try to end the letter with a positive promise to your loved one – that you will do something in their memory, achieve a personal goal for them, maintain their grave or even pause to think of them on their anniversary.

7. Attend a grief support group

When it comes to grief support, we initially tend to look at it very much as 'I don't need help – I can do this on my own'. Some men even adopt the view that it is somehow not manly to deal with emotions in a group setting. All that view achieves is to deprive them of one of the most powerful supports available: that of the human family. Group support is very much what it says on the tin; everyone involved gets to benefit. All you have to do is to be willing to try. So why not give it a go?

Identify a grief support group in your area – or outside your area if you are more comfortable – and attend a meeting. Your doctor, local church minister or citizens advice centre should have contact details.

Keep an open mind when you attend, and try to identify and not compare. You don't have to share your emotions or loss at your very first meeting – listening is your primary objective. But it will help if you are able to speak a little about what you have lost. Doing so will ease your entry into the group.

Remember that the healing power is in the group. You may go hoping for help for yourself, but the reality is that by simply attending and participating honestly you are helping others as much as yourself, and you will also meet new people.

8. Be a guardian of your shared experiences

This should *only* be attempted when you feel you are ready for it. The exercise is not to be rushed or forced.

Take a photograph of the loved one you have lost, perhaps from a framed picture or a photograph in an album. Study the person in the photograph and, in your mind, list the five things you loved most about them. If it helps, try to think of special memories that best define each aspect of their personality, things about them only known to you.

Think about the times you shared, the memories you forged together and how much better your lives were for being lived together. Now think about what your loved one would want for you, for your future. Would they want you living a life mired in grief and sadness? Would you want that for them?

Those qualities about them that you listed and the memories you forged together are now in your guardianship. Consider that to keep them alive and fresh, you need to now live your own life. You owe it not just to yourself but to your loved one.

9. Take an inventory

Everyone benefits from timely housekeeping – and I'm not talking about hoovering your home incessantly or ironing everything from shirts to underwear and curtains. This exercise is all about a personal inventory, to ensure that the things that surround us are as positive as possible and help us to process our grief.

Take careful note of your home and surroundings. While it is important to retain reminders of our lost loved ones, it may not be healthy for us in the long run to have a home that more resembles a shrine than a healthy living space.

How many photographs of your loved one are on walls, tables and mantelpieces? Do you think they are all necessary? Or perhaps would just a few favourite photographs in a special place suffice?

Have you a wardrobe of their clothes and shoes lovingly kept since the day they passed? Perhaps consider keeping one or two special outfits and donating the remainder to charity in your loved one's name. I had some household items like blankets and cushions made from clothing. Maybe allow special friends and relatives to select outfits as a personal 'thank you' if they have been of great support.

Is it the same with perfumes and aftershaves? Why not consider keeping a bottle of their favourite scent as a personal memento and then sharing the rest between relatives and loved ones, again in your loved one's name?

The reason behind all of this is that it can be very hard to process grief if you live every day of your life in what is effectively a mausoleum. No one is saying you should erase your loved one from your life. I have a friend who uses their mother's photo as the screensaver on their computer and as a token on their keychain. But their house has just a few specially chosen photos, and all their mother's clothes were donated to charity.

10. *Set goals*

I believe the key to life is purpose – that is what makes the difference between existing and living. By setting goals for ourselves, by challenging ourselves, we bring positivity into our lives and suddenly have a forward direction. Nothing damages the human spirit more than apathy and idleness.

Make a list of five things you always wanted to do but never have, then take your courage in your hands and set a rough date to achieve them. This is not a bucket list. Rather, it is a life list to help you get busy living. And if it helps, dedicate achieving them to your lost loved one. These should be things you always want to do – and not things that someone else has suggested you should do.

The very best things to list are positive or development goals. For instance, have you ever wanted to learn a few words of a new language to visit a city you've always dreamed about? Or perhaps you could learn a new skill.

Maybe you've always wanted to trek a pilgrimage route like the Camino de Santiago and take time for personal reflection en route? Or to sing in a choir? Or to go back to education to study for a third-level qualification? Do you like reading? Why not set yourself a goal of reading a list of 'The 100 Greatest Books Ever Written' – and join a book club to discuss them?

Try not to have your goals money-related, and if your list involves spin-off benefits for others, all the better.

ACKNOWLEDGEMENTS

Tracey

To my late mother, Rita; father, John; sister, Marilyn; brother, Wayne; and other family members who are always there for me. I wouldn't be half the person I am without your love and support.

To my husband, Dave – my companion and very best friend – you are the most selfless and giving man. I love you.

To Ralph Riegel, who never fails to remind me of what good there is in the world. I am lucky to have met you. Where I scribble a mismatched jumble of words, it is you who disentangles and reorders them to give my voice some finesse! Your patience and conviviality are a balm to the mind.

To everyone at Gill Books for having such faith in this project and for being so sensitive with the manuscript. Special mention must go to the wonderful Sarah Liddy, Kristin, Chloe, Laura, Charlie, Paul and Aoibheann. I would also like to thank all those at Gill Books whom I haven't yet had the pleasure of meeting but whose contribution is evident, essential and very much appreciated.

I will be eternally grateful to Terry Prone, Barry McElhone and Aileen Gaskin at the Communications Clinic, who have provided such valuable advice.

To all of you who continue to support me and for your support of the Jason's Journey pages, thank you for doing so much to raise awareness of the case and associated issues since 2015. I am forever in your debt.

To Nuala Galvin for her tireless work on the 'Bring Justice for Jason' social media page. I remain inspired by your posts. This page is not big enough to convey what your love and support has given me during the most awful of times. You are my guardian angel.

I would also like to express my deepest gratitude to the many people who saw me through difficult times in my life; to all those who provided support on social media; those who came along as I tried out new things – like sea swimming, meditation, yoga, sailing and walking – to help me cope and heal.

Thank you to the many kind and caring people who provide support services that help people through such their most challenging times. I have included a list of contacts in this book.

Special thanks to my friends who have been by my side all my life and those who have entered it recently. The solidarity and support I have during my fight for justice for my brother Jason has been the backbone of my resilience.

To my four wonderful children – Dean, Adam, Jack and Sarah – my daughter-in-law, Kelly, and baby grandson, Max. Together we have consciously tried to make every new day an adventure, and, in the process, we have helped to heal one another. Your resilience, strength, courage, love and determination are inspiring. I love you all!

Lastly, I would like to thank those who have died whom I loved, not least Jason and my mother, Rita, for all the memories, the laughs and your 'can do' glass-half-full attitude. I was so lucky that you were in my life. It is a gift I will treasure forever;

in death you continue to teach me how to be the best version of myself.

I would like to dedicate this book to all of you who have been bereaved by the death of a loved one. May time allow you the resilience to create experiences to ease the pain of the death of your loved ones. Their lives and spirits will continue to live within us.

Ralph

Thanks to Gill Books for their support of this project and I am very grateful to Sarah Liddy for all her faith in it.

Thanks also to Tracey Corbett-Lynch for once again entrusting me with her book – it was a pleasure to work together again.

Special mention to Aoibheann Molumby and Kristen Olson for all their work in supporting the project.

Thanks also to Kieran Kelly for his expert legal advice.

This project would not have been possible without the help, support and understanding of my colleagues at Independent News & Media. Special mention to Gareth Morgan, Rory Tevlin, Alan Caulfield, Breda Heffernan, Eva Gibney, Paul Sheridan, Fionnán Sheahan, Denise Calnan, Ryan Nugent, Luke Byrne, Cormac Bourke, Alan Steenson and Alan English.

On a personal note, my wife, Mary, and children, Rachel, Rebecca and Ralph, as well as my mother, Nora, were staunch supporters as always. I am very grateful for their help and understanding as I vanished for days on end to research and write material for this book.

RESOURCES

Bereavement Support

Irish Hospice Foundation

Charity dedicated to all matters
relating to dying, death and
bereavement in Ireland.
Freephone (1800) 807 077 10 a.m. to
1 p.m., Monday to Friday;
www.hospicefoundation.ie

The Samaritans

Provides emotional support to anyone
in emotional distress, struggling to
cope, or at risk of suicide.
Contact jo@samaritans.ie; Freephone
116 123 anytime; text 50808;
www.samaritans.org

Bereavement support for parents and families

Anam Cara

Provides parental and sibling
bereavement support.
Phone (01) 4045378 or (085) 288
8888; www.anamcara.ie

Féileacáin

Provides support to anyone affected
by the death of a baby during or after
pregnancy.
Phone (028) 51301 and (085)
2496464; www.feileacain.ie

Pregnancy and Infant Loss Ireland

A directory of support services and
knowledge for both bereaved parents
and healthcare professionals.
www. pregnancyandinfantloss.ie

FirstLight

Provides free professional support
and information to families in Ireland
that have experienced the sudden,
unexpected death of their child.
Phone (1800) 391 391;
www.firstlight.ie

A Little Lifetime Foundation

Provides supports and services to
parents whose baby has died around
the time of birth or shortly afterwards
and parents who receive a diagnosis of
fatal foetal abnormality in pregnancy.
Phone (01) 8829030;
www.alittlelifetime.ie

Supports for bereaved children

Children's Grief Centre, Limerick

Support service for children who
have experienced a loss through
bereavement, separation or divorce.
Phone (061) 224627;
www.childrensgriefcentre.ie

Barnardos

Charity supporting children and parents.
Phone (01) 473 2110 10 a.m. to 12 p.m., Monday to Thursday; www.barnardos.ie

Childline

Childline is Ireland's 24-hour national listening service for all children and young people (under the age of 18) in Ireland.
Freephone (1800) 666 666 24/7; text 50101 10 a.m. to 4 p.m. every day; www.childline.ie

The Irish Childhood Bereavement Network

A network for those working with bereaved children and young people and their families.
www.childhoodbereavement.ie

Rainbows

A free, voluntary service for children and young people experiencing loss following bereavement and parental separation.
www.rainbowsireland.ie

Supports for people bereaved by a suicide

HUGG

Offers support groups for anyone over 18 who has been bereaved by suicide.
www.hugg.ie

Pieta

Pieta provides free counselling to individuals who have been bereaved by suicide.
Freephone (1800) 247 247 anytime; text HELP to 51444; www.pieta.ie

The Suicide Bereavement Liaison Service

Free, confidential service that provides assistance and support after the loss of a loved one to suicide. The liaison officer can meet with a bereaved family as a group or individually. This service is provided by pieta. ie (nationwide), vitahouse.org (Roscommon) and thefamilycentre. com (Mayo).

General counselling

Contact your local Health Service Executive office or Primary Care Centre. Information on counselling is also available from the Irish Association for Counselling and Psychotherapy (IACP), the Irish Association of Humanistic and Integrative Psychotherapy and the Psychological Society of Ireland (PSI).